PRIMAL METHOD

A Systematic Approach To Preparedness
For The Modern Age

Everything You Need To Know To Get Further
Faster In Life, And Go From Average To
Savage In Your Preparedness, Without Having
To Navigate The Traditional Rivers Of Bullsh!t,
And Get Paid In The Process!

Written By:
Ian "Primal" Talbert

"The Primal Method"

For bulk events, bookstores, or wholesale ordering
information, please contact the author directly at
ian@primaloptics.com.

www.primaloptics.com   www.masktactical.com

PRIMAL

ISBN: 9798674200499

DEDICATION

I dedicate this book to my 4 true loves.

To God, whose mighty guiding light helps me create things that have substantial positive impacts on people's lives. Thank you for blessing me with your wisdom and a beautiful, loving family.

To my wife, Cora, for without your loyalty, push, and support during the endless grind that is entrepreneurship, none of my creations, including this book, would have ever happened. Thank you for believing in my crazy endeavors, being an incredible mother, and for providing me two beautiful kids.

To my daughter, Rowan, for it was your birth that sparked my sincere desire to become the best man I can be. I didn't know what love was until the day you were born, which changed me for the better. Thank you for filling my heart with joy and fueling my fire for creation.

Lastly, to my son, Tank. Who's passion and curiosity for adventure keeps me feeling younger than I am and happier than I deserve. Thank you for continually reminding me of how exciting life can be. I know you're going to do great things for the world.

CONTENTS

FOREWORD

Written By: Eddie Debus
Business Owner / Personal Trainer / Fitness Pro

So what can I say about the Primal Method? Well, the first thing is that it's not a typical prepper course or survival training program. It's an effective strategy for total life preparedness. When you think of a "prepper," what comes to mind? Probably someone who hoards a bunch of weapons and food for the worst-case scenario, right? Ian's method isn't anything like that.

You will see that truth in just the first part of the program. The focus on finance, family, and fitness and the balance of them. What does being "prepared" matter when your finances or family life are in total disarray? It means you're not prepared. If you have all the weapons and food stores possible, it won't help you if you're broke, miserable, and in bad physical shape.

The very beginning of The Primal Method sets it apart from any other program alone. It highlights the things nobody seems to address. What he has shed light on in just two layers of his multi-faceted program is enough to change your life NOW. Imagine nothing catastrophic ever happens? Are you going to be better or worse, or the same, which is also worse, or is your life going to be different?

The whole process is here. Family fitness, financial fitness, and physical fitness are the starting points. Without these nailed down, anything else you do is next to useless.

I've been a personal trainer for everyone from house moms to pro fighters for nearly a decade, and guess what? Even for professionals, financial and family fitness make a massive difference in their physical training. You can be the greatest fighter or bodybuilder in the world, but if your family or financial fitness is off, it's going to show in your training. You will underperform. It's all about being well rounded.

You might think pouring everything into one aspect means success, and it might, but only in that one aspect.

This method aims at optimizing all aspects of life. If it didn't, I wouldn't have bought into it as I have.

The Primal Method is something I got on board with because it's full-spectrum life. It's not some course on how to just prep. It's a course on how to change your mindset and your life—prepping overall, not the norm, which lacks the substance to make the difference.

I highly recommend The Primal Method because it will indeed make the difference so long as you do the work that's asked of you.

SPECIAL DEDICATION

To Eddie, you were such an incredible influence on my life and so many others. Although we didn't grow up together, we developed a brotherly bond that felt no different than if we had in the short few years we knew each other. I speak for many when I say we all love and miss you dearly. You will always be my coach, mentor, and friend. We had many plans, and I promise I will continue to carry the torch and carry out our mission. I know you wouldn't have it any other way. You and your family will always be close in my heart and prayers.

We will reunite one day, my savage brother.

EDDIE DEBUS

Rest In Peace

INTRODUCTION

The Primal Method is a method; it's merely a way to train. Not a training itself. It's a system that you apply to the overall preparedness strategy designed to prepare you for the modern age and the highest priority threats first.

One of the most significant issues I have seen in people's preparedness plans is that they are spending loads of time, money, and energy on aspects that help overall, but rarely where it matters most.

I'm specifically speaking to areas of your life that present the biggest threats to your survival. Unfortunately, most folks I meet are doing just that, preparing backward for the lowest priority threats first.

Where you are genuinely weakest skill-wise might be primitive bushcraft, but where your survival is most at risk might be self-defense or fitness; therefore, it makes more sense to focus on those layers of preparedness first.

Survival is the goal, not merely looking or feeling cool. That means the order of operations should be strategic, and that, my friend, is what led me towards the creation of my method.

The first thing to do is identify what is threatening your survival most right now, and that's where you should dial in your focus. Not necessarily where you are weakest overall. However, it can undoubtedly be the same thing.

People need a practical way to prepare for modern age threats, and after searching all over for years to fulfill my own needs, I never found a system that made much sense. That's when I started to develop ideas of my own.

I wanted to create a system that anyone could follow. Something people could use regardless of where or whom they source their training.

It doesn't matter if it's Billy Bob on Youtube, Prepper Pete down the street, or a professional instructor and training academy.

You can apply the Primal Method, and this book will tell you what it is and why you need to be using it as the foundation for your life and preparedness as a whole.

Throughout this journey, I will curse, be abrasive at times, and possibly piss you off with some of the things I challenge you to do or understand.

If this worries you, this might not be the book for you.

However, if a change is what you truly seek, If preparedness is your ultimate goal, take this ride with me. I promise when we reach our destination, you will step out of this car with a completely re-engineered perspective about life.

I designed this method to help you reach optimal preparedness levels and get you further much faster than you would typically be able to.

I will teach you how to get prepared, get the life you want, and even explain how you can get paid to do it. That's right; I'm going to teach you how to get paid to get prepared and pursue everything you want in life.

This type of lifestyle generally comes pre-programmed with rivers of bullshit to navigate. I want to give you the blueprint to avoid these rivers and teach you tactics that will help you perform to the best of your abilities in all aspects of your life. All of this might sound like fancy rhetoric, but it's not, and I am confident that when we conclude this journey, you'll see that light too.

I've spent the majority of my life as somewhat of a guinea pig, testing theories, and one thing I've noticed is that the landscape for preparedness has evolved dramatically and rapidly over the years. The things we prepare for today are much different than that of our ancestors. Threats evolve, and therefore it only makes sense that our strategy to combat them should adapt too.

Unfortunately, I don't believe we've seen parallel evolution in that department, which seems to ring true in most things. The "don't reinvent the wheel" concept, while sound in many ways, also puts blinders on innovation. It's a real creativity buzz kill, to be honest. I think we have shot ourselves in the foot at scale.

I think because of this design, many people will always struggle to combat their enemies. You need to be innovative if you want long term success at this.

"Enemies" are anything or anyone that stands between you and your objectives. It might be an emotion, a limiting belief, or flat out someone who wants to kill you. If we want to maintain the element of surprise, If we're going to keep the upper hand on these enemies, I think it's vital to follow the clues and stick to what's tried and true to get consistently positive results.

However, it's equally important to frequently embrace our creativity to keep life interesting and keep our enemies guessing. It's challenging to do this unless we reinvent the wheel from time to time.

The Primal Method is a systematic approach to preparedness for the modern age. When people wake up to the prepared lifestyle, they often start with their priorities backward.

Preparedness is much more than knowing how to build fires and primitive shelters, it's much more than having many weapons and gear, and it's much more than having years of food and water storage. To be prepared for the modern age, you need to be strategic, and The Primal Method is your blueprint for proper preparedness.

None of the gear, none of the skills, none of the plans mean anything if you come home to a life you're not happy to live, and this is where The Primal Method starts. To be ready for tough times in life, you need to have a solid foundation to build your skills and knowledge, and that's why we focus on that foundation in layer one of the method. I want The Primal Method to help you get prepared for the highest priority things in life.

Think of it as your preparedness bible.

Before we dive into the meat and potatoes, I want you first to get to know me a little, and I want to teach you the underlying theory behind The Primal Method. The method itself isn't all that complicated.

Understanding the reasoning for it will take more time than learning what the method is itself, but you must pay close attention, and I promise you won't regret it when we're finished.

So, let's take this journey together . . .

. . . Are you ready?

NICE TO MEET YOU

Who Is Ian "Primal" Talbert?

The keyboard has become an integral weapon in modern age warfare. Words are powerful. I aim to use them in ways that inspire action, garner the plaudits of critics, and persuade adamant minds about doing better.

Action is king; it gets the job done. Words are the queen of influence that ensures the job gets done right. I bear a sword for when violence is the only answer, but I also carry parchment and pen when the enemy is more than an arm's length away.

I will always attempt to use words to persuade my enemies into becoming my allies, and my allies into becoming great people with huge hearts and an immense capacity for infectious positivity.

For those that genuinely desire growth, I hope my words can help you achieve it.

For those that stand against, well, there is always the sword.

I'm not a keyboard warrior.

I am a warrior with a keyboard.

There's a significant difference.

"The state that separates its scholars from its warriors will have its thinking done by cowards and its fighting done by fools." - Thucydides

In the future, I may very well write an autobiography, but this is not it. You're here to learn about this magical method, not so much about me, so we'll keep the intro short and sweet.

I was born on January 17th, 1992, on Fort Knox. I am the owner of MASK Tactical, founder of The Warrior Tribe, and creator of The Primal Method to preparedness. I have also served in the military as an Infantryman in the Army National Guard, built businesses, and pursued many things.

I've been in a lot of challenging situations, but we all have life struggles. Some more than others, but I'm not going to give you a big list of lessons from my life in this particular book. I have many life lessons that I'd love to share, but that's for another time.

However, I will inject a handful of my most impactful journal entries along the way, but right now, I want to teach you something that will alter your life forever and for the better should you choose to implement it.

When I got out of the military, I discovered a big void in my life, and something didn't feel right. I couldn't place my finger on it for the longest time, and I searched far and wide for a solution, but after years of hunting, I finally decided to take matters into my own hands and create the answers I needed.

It turns out many other folks came to realize they had this same void and desired the same solutions too.

Before joining the military, I had already tasted entrepreneurship. I knew I had a fierce passion for it already, and the military helped me get back to my love for preparedness and the great outdoors. So naturally, I decided to combine my business goals with my life goals, and one of my life goals is to become 10x more prepared than everyone around me.

To achieve that, I know that I must also train 10x as hard as everyone else, which isn't possible with a regular job. A typical 9-5 won't cut it. I knew I had to revolve my career around it for this goal to be realistic.

That's when M.A.S.K. Tactical was born.

Several years later, The Warrior Tribe, and several years after that, I conceived The Primal Method. I am writing this book to show you exactly how and why all these things matter if you have similar goals for preparedness, success, happiness, or wealth. It all starts with what I call the. . .

. . . Fallacy of Balance.

PRIMAL'S WAR JOURNAL

DATE: SEPT. 3RD 2014
SUBJECT: MOJO

Your "Mojo" isn't going to just come back.

That moment you're waiting on to feel good enough to do something about it isn't coming either. You just have to get up and go capture it.

Dr. Evil isn't just going to hand it back all because you're tired of being the nail in life. Stop feeling sorry for yourself because nobody else does when it boils down to it.

Pick up the fucking hammer, and start driving the nails.

SECTION I: THE FALLACY OF BALANCE

CHAPTER 1

The Trifecta Of "F" Words

How the idea of achieving balance on the mountain's side is restricting your ability to make it to the apex.

The idea of balance between Family, Fitness, and Finances is something we humans crave more than anything. We've pursued it since the dawn of time.

Go ask your friends what they genuinely want, and I bet most of them will say, "I'd just be happy to have some stability."

So, here's a diagram to help you visualize what this delicate balance looks like. If you're anything like me, visuals can help quite a bit.

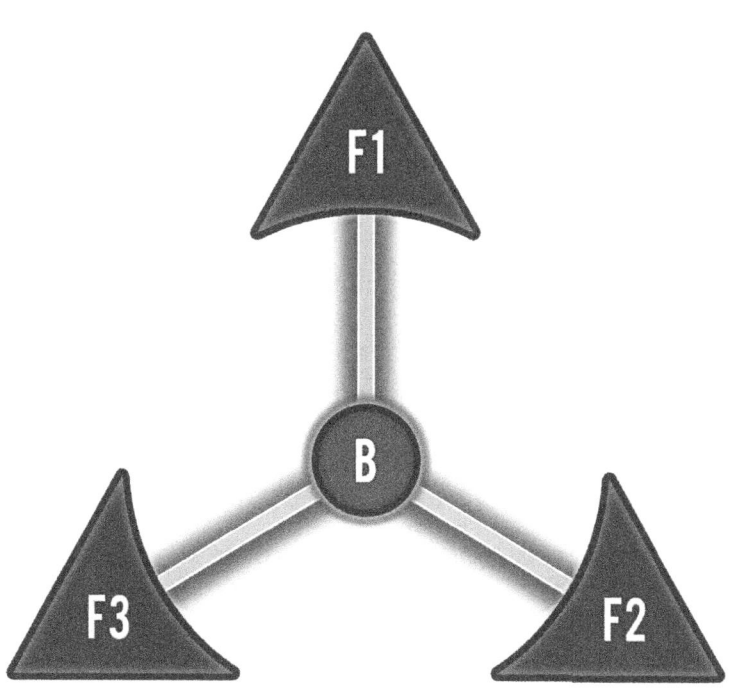

F1 = FAMILY   **F3 = FINANCE**

F2 = FITNESS   **B = BALANCE**

Everyone wants balance. It just feels right. Feeling "balance" is a feeling like no other. No drug or drink compares to the high we get when life feels perfectly in tune with our soul, and nothing sucks more than when it's not.

We used to experience this feeling frequently growing up when life was simple, but we create more interference between heart, mind, body, and soul as we evolve. Ignorant of the fact we are ultimately the architect of our demise.

I've found that very few people possess the ability to understand this dynamic—the gift of self-awareness. I call it a gift because while it is teachable to a low degree, you typically either have it or don't. However, there are certain cases where one day, all of a sudden, people wake up.

I know this because I am one of those people. I had virtually no trace of self-awareness growing up, then one day, out of what seemed like nowhere, I felt wise as a wizard. It wasn't random, though, and feeling it isn't enough. I have to validate it, I told myself. So I started taking new actions to prove it.

At first, I couldn't put my finger on it. This new perspective feels excellent, but what woke me up? What can I attribute this enlightenment too? Nothing this profound is random, right?

It took a while to figure it out, but there's a particular reason why this wake up occurs, and many people are entirely unaware of it. We'll talk more about this reason later, though, as there's more pre-framing you and I need to do right now. You need to be primed with the Primal theory before you receive this method to employ it properly.

My hope for this book and what I have created with The Primal Method is to position you to a systematic perspective about life in such a way that it triggers newfound self-awareness. I hope the intel in this book provides you with as big of an epiphany moment as it did for me. Once I put all these pieces together, my life improved in every aspect. My preparedness and understanding of it have dramatically improved and changed as well. When it finally hit me, I woke up to a startling fact that showed me how backward we have indeed become.

That fact was that I and many others had been living the prepared life focused on the wrong side of the spectrum.

For a long time, The Primal Method stewed in the back of my mind. For nearly a decade, there were many gray areas that I hadn't quite figured out yet. It made it all hard to understand and even harder to explain. Deep down, this grand vision of mine was rooted for a long time, but it wasn't until about 2017 that it was stimulated in just the right way for it to grow, and I was finally able to gather all the variables to the equation.

I knew it was there; I just couldn't get it all dialed in. But I knew it was there, and that belief ultimately kept me focused long enough to figure it out. You see, I failed at school, like, miserably. Specifically, in mathematics, you can bet your ass that I never did my homework or solved problems in class, but this was the one equation in the test of life that I took home, analyzed, and attempted to answer every single day.

THE EQUATION OF "BALANCE."

The great thing is that once you're aware of all the variables, the equation becomes easier to solve. The challenge is that we've built a society that likes to shield us from these variables.

We don't become enlightened until we breach beyond our self-made prisons, and to do so, we must first inform ourselves that it exists. We built it, and we hold the key. Self-awareness, remember? Without it, the prison becomes all we can see.

Once we can no longer see the exterior, the interior eventually becomes all we know. The only thing that brings back that knowledge of the outside world is a tragedy that reminds us of how painful it is when we're no longer in the pursuit of happiness. When we choose to settle for less than that, we get stale. When that happens, our self-awareness diminishes.

In short, without self-awareness, life is and always will be more of a challenge for you.

So, there are 24 hours in a day, and if we assume, 8 hours are always devoted to sleep, 16 hours a day is what remains. For most of us, we'll divide that time between the trifecta of "F" words (Family, Fitness, and Finances) until we feel in harmony.

This is great. After all, it's what we desired.

It feels so amazing, until one day it doesn't.

CHAPTER 2

The Facade

We must dive deep into the depths of our soul and shed some light on the darkness. The surface level is not where you will achieve the balance or greatness you crave.

Life? Life is a fighter.

It's always ready to throw down, and it doesn't care about your balance. See, while you fixate on achieving this balance you crave, you fail to keep your eyes on your opponent, and down comes Wreck-It Ralph sized hammer fists against your unprepared facade.

Thus begins your first ride on the rollercoaster of life, and don't be stupid enough to think you're only going to ride it once.

The longer you try to build up the facade, the more punches life's going to throw, and you're going to eat them every time because you're not focused on fighting but rather this idea of balance.

The facade is this opaque surface-level attempt to convince ourselves and those who witness that we genuinely have our shit together behind the walls we build. For me, I like transparency. Fuck a facade. I want my depth to feel as good as I display it on the surface. I like to be transparent as it helps keep me honest, accountable, and focused on what matters most, the inside.

The only problem with being transparent and lowering that guard is that life can hit you easier. However, once you truly understand how this algorithm of balance works, you'll effectively defend yourself against the enemy.

Remember, *"Enemies are anything or anyone that stands between you and your objectives."*

Now, some people have successfully achieved balance, and that's because they understand how this algorithm works, but most people don't, and they spend their entire lives chasing it and failing.

It's a fallacy. This idea of balance during the climb up life's mountain, I've discovered, is the culprit behind most people's challenges of actually achieving it for the long term. Balance is a destination, **not** a decoration that we can hang up in our lives whenever we please.

Sustainably balancing on the climb up life's mountain is near impossible, but you can balance at the apex, and it's only at the top should you spend your time trying to do so.

It's counterproductive otherwise.

CHAPTER 3

The Weight Limit

The ultimate breaking point that forces you to decide your fate. Arriving here just may lead to the most pivotal moment of your life. However, hitting this point isn't an ideal situation, so don't wait until it happens. There's a chance you won't make it out alive.

If you focus on finding balance during the climb, you will find yourself off the trail, taking the wrong actions, and traversing further away from the summit. The worst part is, you won't even realize it because you'll still feel like you're in pursuit of the same goal. That is, of course, until you hit your weight limit.

Hitting this weight limit can get you re-focused, but it could also kill you.

Remember that reason for waking up we talked about earlier? That's the weight limit. We all have one that's unique to us, and genuinely hitting your mental weight limit has two possible outcomes: suicide or self-awareness. If there's a third option to persevere, you know you're not at your weight limit yet.

I've found many people to be exceptionally proficient at skirting the edge of rock bottom, though. Staying just out of range, but not much farther. Often, unfortunately, for their entire lives. You might get good at carrying all this pressure, you might be great at suffering, but in the end, you can only get so strong, and there is no shortage of weight.

Hitting it means you are done being in pain, and you are either genuinely ready to throw in the towel or get back in the fight and dominate with a new perspective. If you aren't at your limit, you may stay in the fight, but with the same outlook, all you will experience is more of the same. Rock bottom doesn't have to be what wakes you up. It just helps those of us who are too stubborn. You can decide right here and now to change the way you look at things.

You have to turn the lights on.

Flipping this switch requires you to change the way you perceive suffering because it's not going anywhere. Instead of it being hard and painful, view it as the only way to grow and learn to become comfortable being uncomfortable.

Jordan Peterson says, *"Life is suffering, but you have the power to transcend it."*

You need to transform suffering in your mind from the bad guy to your best friend. When you seek out discomfort, instead of running from it, it has a strange but positive effect on the mental weight you carry. It clears the fog and helps you navigate rough terrain. Want balance? Seek suffering, don't run from it or try to hack your way around it.

When you develop this outlook, challenging situations start to look more like bridges to greener pastures than roadblocks or setbacks. So, let's talk more about this weight limitation. You see, much like when we go to the gym and lift weights, we're mentally lifting weights daily.

Let's use the bench press as an example.

We've all tried it at least once.

In the gym, a standard bar usually has a default weight of 45 lbs. Much like physically benching, our mind carries around default weight as well. The only difference is that it doesn't take a rest between sets. In fact, it never really rests at all.

The beginning of this set started the day we were born and will end the day we die. Fortunately, when it comes to bench pressing physically, we can put that bar and all the weight down and take a break.

Our *mind*, however, isn't so lucky.

As I said, there's always a default amount of weight we will never be able to escape, but this doesn't mean we can't mitigate how much weight we're carrying around. Unlike physically bench pressing, where the goal is to lift a lot of weight, our goal with mental weightlifting is to remove as much weight from the bar of life as possible.

When physically benching, you know that once you put one too many plates on that bar, it's going to crush your trachea.

Mental benching is no different.

Too much weight will crush and possibly kill you either way.

This discovery eventually leads me to a pivotal realization that many people like to talk about as a problem, yet they rarely invest in or create solutions.

I am a solutions-oriented guy, so I did what I do.

I went to work on solving the problem.

If not you, then who, right?

PRIMAL'S WAR JOURNAL

DATE: AUG. 6TH 2013
SUBJECT: RELENTLESS ACTION

I'm going to create a significant change in the world. I can feel it as sure as Alaska is cold, but I know I must change myself into the kind of leader that's worthy of such a prestigious goal.

I must train, I must learn, I must focus.

I must **take relentless action**.

I must get uncomfortable.

I must never negotiate with what must be done.

SECTION II: THREAT ASSESSMENT

CHAPTER 4

The Disproportionate Threats

Add all the likely threats together that are controllable, and they'll still fall short of the danger we pose to ourselves. We have to stop ignoring it. We also need to stop using the cool aspects of preparedness as escapism in the same way some resort to drugs or alcohol. The foundation must be stable, or none of it matters at the end of the day. The biggest threats are directly under our nose.

Short of diseases and accidental injuries, suicide is one of the biggest threats to our survival today. More so than an active shooter, a home invader, a natural disaster, or terrorist attack. Your physical and mental health should always be a priority when it comes to your preparedness. If you want to eliminate potential threats to your survival, it only makes sense that you start where you're most vulnerable.

These are the most concerning things at scale, according to the data. The better your physical body is, the better your brain will operate. Both physical and psyche play the game hand in hand, but in my opinion, everything begins and ends in the mind. Therefore, ground zero starts with getting your mindset clear and correct. You then go on to enhance it through your physical fitness.

If you're strong enough mentally, you can tune out pain and convince your body to persevere past your wildest imagination. How else do you think guys like David Goggins can run 200+ miles without stopping? Of course, there's tons of training, but it's the mental discipline that makes this possible. They're not superhumans; they're simply masters of their minds.

If the mind is weak, it will tell the body to stop when it feels pain. If it's strong, it can persuade the body to do some incredible things despite it.

Although we don't have a cure for everything, we know a lot about combating diseases at this point and being physically fit will undoubtedly help you mitigate adverse health conditions. However, we can't completely control this at the end of the day.

Next is accidental injury/death, which we can mitigate by training situational awareness and playing it safe, but we can't totally control this either.

The first significant threat we can completely control is intentional harm (suicide), and it's a huge issue.

According to the data, it's a grossly disproportionate threat, but it's one that we can indeed control.

This is obvious, and it goes without saying, but what isn't apparent are the solutions for combating it. Because it's such a subjective threat, it's tough to create solutions that help massive amounts of people.

Everyone has a different *"weight limit,"* remember?

So, *"how do you cure suicide?"*

This was the question I began asking myself when The Primal Method concept was finally starting to take shape and reveal it's full glory.

The goal was to become 10x more prepared than anyone around me. Consequently, this begged the question...

"What is the biggest threat to my survival?"

When I discovered that suicide is statistically more likely to kill me than almost everything most *"preppers"* prepare for combined, I knew my perspective needed to shift.

Of course, other threats need to be analyzed. Just because the stats tell us that suicide kills more people doesn't mean that you're not closer to a different threat. However, if you don't find that you are, you should focus on the whole, and when you do that, suicide becomes the highest-ranking controllable threat. Once I identified this flaw in my preparedness, I noticed it trend in nearly everyone else who lives the *"prepared"* life.

The sad part about all of this, though, is that it seems like most people have to be the victim of something catastrophic before they wake up to the idea of living prepared.

You should never wait for that to happen.

It's vital that when you do wake up, that you follow an approach that gets you prepared for the highest priority threats in life first.

Now, before you think it and then say it, yes, it's all relative. Person (A) may very well be less likely to commit suicide than person (B), or person (C) might be more likely to die by a flash flood than person (D).

Everyone's priorities for survival are different, but generally speaking, there are specific threats such as suicide, diseases, and more that happen to have a much higher statistical likelihood across the board.

I have this big vision to impact and change a massive amount of lives for the better, so the next questions became...

"How can I save the most lives?" and then, logically, *"Well, how can I cure suicide?"*

It's such a bold goal, I know. What I really meant by *"cure"* is, what solutions can I create to put a severe dent in this issue?

I told myself, *"If I could save more people from disease and suicide, I would be able to save more people's lives and make this impact way easier than if I were to only focus on the "cool stuff" when it comes to preparedness."*

Everyone I've ever asked, when they hear the words *survival* or *preparedness*, their minds default to bushcrafting or stocking up years of supplies.

Not one person has told me they think about their life's foundational aspects. Modern society has trained us to disassociate those things in this lifestyle.

When I say *"foundations,"* what I'm talking about are the aspects of your life that remain when you peel back all the fancy layers of preparedness, such as your career, relationships, finances, and goals. These things are practically your backbone for life, and I think you know it's essential to take care of your spine.

Now, I'm not saying that primitive skills, self-defense training, or supplies prepping are bad. Not at all. That would be preposterous. They are vital to the process, but for most people, they begin their preparedness journey at the wrong end, spending tons of time, energy, and money training and learning things that do indeed matter, just not in relation to their more significant threats.

It's our fault this happens, though.

We designed a system that fails to prepare us for real life. It doesn't teach us about survival priorities. It teaches us how to live an enslaved life. We left people to their own devices, and in today's age, those devices are typically Google and Youtube from their smartphones.

Today, people can hop online, type in how to get prepared, and lo and behold, Bushcraft Bob's YouTube Channel pops up.

Heck, maybe they even know Prepper Pete down the street. This isn't totally a bad thing. Pete and Bob might both have some great content. Statistically, probably not, but hey, you got lucky, and they're both pros. They're frequently not, though, and most people aren't as fortunate as you, and this is where they get kick-started with a checklist slammed full of terrible advice.

Almost always, the first step of preparedness people stumble into is that they need to create a bug out bag and get tons of gear for it.

After that, they go back to Prepper Pete and ask, "What's next, Pete? What do I need now?"

"Guns! You need an arsenal!" Pete says.

So, they go to their local gun shop and stock up on all the guns and ammo they can afford.

Because their source of preparedness knowledge sucks, they invest more of their money into fancy ammo and accessories for their weapons than they do into their training. Because, well, fuck training, it's more important to look the part, right?

Wrong, dead wrong, but the problem is that Prepper Pete and Bushcraft Bob have them convinced that that's how you should prepare for the modern age. Remember, before this person woke up to this lifestyle, they didn't know much about it, and to them, Bushcraft Bob and Prepper Pete look like the epitome of preparedness because they don't know any better.

The educational system failed.

It didn't inform appropriately on this subject, remember?

Now, some people possess enough deductive reasoning skills and common sense to find their way to a good foundation of preparedness. They check their sources and put two and two together. That's only some people, though.

The overwhelming majority don't, and more and more people are killing themselves and becoming more at risk for suicide and diseases every day because of this.

I'm not going to claim that I have created **THE CURE** for suicide because that would be silly. However, suppose one can understand every aspect of The Primal Method and leverage it in combination with our tribe and programs. In that case, they will know how they can mitigate the risk in what I believe is the most effective way possible.

It's a multi-faceted approach, as I'm sure you can already tell. It's not one thing you will do; it's many things, with a strategic order of operations.

So, at this point, with preparedness as the ultimate goal, I determined that suicide prevention and disease mitigation is what I wanted our operation to focus on facilitating at the core. Since they're statistically more likely to happen than almost everything across the board, it became the obvious starting point—the foundational thing we need to prepare for.

Again, everything is relative, so please take a step back and analyze your surroundings. If you live in a war zone, you're probably a little more likely to become a war casualty than a casualty of suicide.

Suicide is a little different than all the other causes of death. We all wake up every day and make decisions. Some might position us into the enemy's field of fire, some of them, the enemy into ours. We do our best to make the right decisions to align us with a victory, but occasionally, we screw it up.

THERE ARE 4 PRIMARY

MANNERS OF DEATH.

1. **Natural**

2. **Accidental**

3. **Homicide**

4. **Suicide**

Every cause of death is a subset of one of those four parent categories. The difference between a manner and cause of death is like the difference between answering a math problem and showing your work.

You remember when the teachers would tell us to show our work, don't you?

The *cause* is the "what," the *manner* is the "how." Both are essential things to know. We need to know the **what** so we can identify the issues, and we need to know the **how**, to determine what we need to do to prevent the problems from even happening.

Every manner of death is avoidable to a degree.

There's always something we can do to lower our risks.

We can eat healthier to lower our risk of heart disease. We can move to a state with lower rates of homicide. We can refrain from crowds to avoid active shooters.

We always seem to tread carefully and heavily invest in preparedness for these types of threats. However, suicide is rarely perceived as a threat in the same way everything else is. When it comes to suicide specifically, people commonly tend to get what I call "alpha ego" about it, especially men.

We tend to get this idea in our heads that we could never be the type of person that would intentionally kill ourselves. Because of this, suicide falls off the threat radar almost entirely, and we neglect to prepare for it in the ways we should, which is an incredibly critical issue.

I liken preparedness for a house.

Without a solid foundation, and over the test of time, mother nature is going to blow it down. If you build your home on a solid foundation, though, it's going to survive a lot longer.

I've conducted this assessment a plethora of times within numerous groups of "*prepared*" individuals.

Every time I do it, I find a large portion focused on *everything but their foundations.*

If there's one thing I've learned from building a large community of prepared minds, it's that many people are royally neglecting life at the core when you peel back all their layers.

People are becoming perpetually concerned with escaping their reality versus fixing it. Fixing problems requires work, and people don't like to work on things for which they lack passion. It's hard to have enthusiasm for anything that doesn't give us the immediate spike of dopamine we crave, but we must if we want to succeed.

Since society has convinced most that chasing passion isn't realistic, most people settle and try to find a job they can tolerate. They become defeated, stagnant in life. Tolerance isn't the only available option, but damn, so many folks act like that's all they have. There is a better way to play the game, and this book is going to explain it.

Look, yes, there's always going to be a pool of dirty jobs that no one wants to do but must be done for the world to function. We're never going to run into the "too many chiefs, not enough Indians." dilemma as a whole, though. By design, we are born, we live, and then we die. Every single day ushers in a new group of Indians who begin at basecamp. There will always be a natural and dramatically disproportionate amount of Indians to chiefs.

It's survival of the fittest, and not everyone makes it to the top. There will always be more people climbing and camping out at ground zero than there will ever be at the summit.

Don't think that you have to stay an Indian your entire life, though, or that you shouldn't encourage others to become a chief for fear of creating too many chiefs.

It's simply never going to happen.

There will always be another climber to fill the void.

We're all born at basecamp, you see, and, as we live, we ascend the mountain hoping to make it to the top before we die. The sooner, the better because the top is the only place on the mountain where we can tap into lasting balance to feel that real light-your-soul-on-fire kind of happiness we desire.

The proper amalgamation of Family, Fitness, and Financials creates a balance accompanied by the highest happiness level you can imagine.

RIDING THE ROLLER COASTER

We taste this balance here and there throughout our ascent, but it never solidifies in our life because of what I call the roller coaster effect. It's the seemingly never-ending series of ups and downs we go through during the climb.

Life is a fighter, remember?

Being that life always wants to throw down. There are a few mental journeys I want you to take with me so that I can explain to you what this roller coaster effect is and how you can avoid it because, let's face it, the roller coaster of life fucking sucks.

It's full of valuable lessons, and you'll never make it to the top without riding it a few times, though. So, it's necessary to the process, but we want to do our best to learn from our mistakes fast and get off the roller coaster as soon as possible to make real progress on our climb.

Every time we take a detour to ride the roller coaster, we delay our happiness.

So, before taking these mental road trips, let's understand the threats a little better.

CHAPTER 5

Getting To The Root

When trying to get rid of a pesky weed, we rip it out from the root. We need to look at solving our problems the same way.

Now that you know just how big a threat suicide is let's dig into it a little deeper. I want to show you why mental and physical fitness needs to be the core foundation of your preparedness.

"*Why do people kill themselves?*" I asked.

Now, there are a lot of different reasons why people decide to end their own lives. Many people will have their own opinions surrounding this, and I am certainly not a psychologist.

Still, I've done my share of research, and I concluded it boils down to stress, depression, and anxiety, specifically stemming from the trifecta of "**F**" words.

Again, those are "***Family, Fitness, and Finances.***"

When any of those core three are out of tune, stress, depression, and anxiety begin to pile upon the mental bar of life. The further out of balance we go, the heavier they weigh, and as I explained earlier, we all have a unique weight limit.

I told you understanding all this theory would be a little more complicated than the method itself, right? I want to phrase some of these concepts in a very universally relatable way to help with that.

Let me give you some examples.

As I break all of this down, I want you to visualize everything I am saying intensely. Can you do that for me, please?

If so, let's take a couple of mental journeys together.

CHAPTER 6

Mental Journeys

A visualization is a powerful tool. Let's use it to understand ourselves on a deeper level.

To start, I want you to imagine a virtually perfect life, a disciplined life. After all, to achieve the dream, it takes a fair degree of discipline. **Wouldn't you agree?**

So, let's take a look at this amazing life you live.

You have the Baywatch body, a career you enjoy and make decent money from, and the relationship you have always dreamed about growing up. You've got the family you always wanted, your favorite dog, the dream car—all of it. You achieved the dream.

Not without struggle, though, of course.

The struggle is not an optional aspect of life; It's a biological requirement responsible for both growth and decline. We can't function without it. We must understand its place and use it as an instrument for said growth, instead of viewing it as a deterrent of happiness.

Precisely, that's what you have done here in this example. You used the struggle to achieve the dream instead of crush it. Seriously, visualize this as vividly as you can. You've cracked the code and won the game.

Visualize this as your very reality right now.

Put yourself in the shoes and your hands on the wheel.

How damn amazing does this life feel? It's everything you ever wanted. Now, let's hop in that dream car with the family and hit the road. Everything's going as planned. The sun's shining, the wind blows in your hair, the birds are chirping the song of freedom, and you get T-boned by a semi-truck.

Suddenly things aren't so beautiful.

You didn't get hurt this time around, but someone you love deeply did.

Everything in life was virtually perfect a few seconds ago. But now, the person you love most in this world is dying right in your arms, and there's not a single fucking thing you can do to stop it. It's happening.

What do you think?

I want you to feel this moment in your bones.

Is this enough weight for you to have the desire to kill yourself? For some people, yes. It's going to depend on how mentally tough and disciplined you are in the face of pain and struggle. However, let's remember, life before this moment was virtually perfect.

Mental toughness and discipline were required to get here. So, is this singular event going to be enough to crush you? Is this it?

I'm sure it will be close, but you will have the best chance to persevere through that pain when you don't have to carry weight in other areas of your life, and right now, you're relatively weightless. You've calloused your mind to harsh conditions. You've persevered through a great deal of pain in your life to get where you are now.

The Family, the Fitness, and Finances.

It took a lot to get this fulfilled life, and now that you don't have to carry around the pressure of broken relationships, bad health, and low finances, the only weight you have to worry about is the unknown. Things you can't control. Like the loss of a loved one.

By default, as I said, there's always going to be a little weight we have to carry—the required struggle. However, suppose you can manage to remove the heaviest weights from the bar. In that case, you'll open up your weight capacity so that when that uncontrollable, devastating event happens, you can navigate it with a higher chance of success.

Now, let's go back into visualization mode and flip the script upside down. Everything is backward now. Life is no longer perfect, and let's face it, this is the reality for so many people.

The truth is, you probably don't have that dream relationship because you have two jobs, and combined, they're still not enough to pay the bills. As a result, you argue all the time, and because of all that negative stress, you eat fast food and never go to the gym. You're steadily getting fat and undesirable day by day. You hate your career; your body is diseased; you're broke and broken.

Life sucks right now. It's the complete opposite of perfection.

Most Americans have less than $600 in the bank if they're lucky. That doesn't stretch very far in the modern age. Here we are, though, with a generally shit life, and you're driving down the same road, and that same semi-truck T-bones you. The person you love the most in the world is, yet again, dying in your arms, and there's nothing you can do about it.

Same scenario, only this time, you're carrying massive weight on the bar of life. Your trifecta of "**F**" words is out of balance, and this causes astronomical amounts of weight to camp upon your shoulders. So much weight that you were already straddling the edge of suicide before the truck hit you. Suddenly, without prior warning to prepare whatsoever, an extra weight outside your control and well beyond your max weight limit is placed onto your bar of life.

Go ahead and guess what the most likely outcome in this situation is?

If you said suicide, you'd be correct.

Life was terrible, remember?

One of the only real lights you had shining in your life was sitting on the side of the car the truck hit. You just watched that light burn out in your arms. At this point, you question if God's light is even real.

However, also at this point, it's only the light of God that can bring you back from depths of this degree.

You have to believe, or that's it. There's no ladder, rope, or human-made otherwise long enough to reach you, only the strong, long arms of God. You may disagree, but you'd be wrong!

(I told you I was abrasive, right? haha!)

In this scenario, you have positioned yourself at considerable risk for the disproportionate threat, suicide.

In this example, before the catastrophe, discipline and mental resilience weren't part of your code of conduct.

Because of this, you may not have the ability to persevere through this level of pain. At least not on your own. Unfortunately, this was more than likely, the nail in your coffin.

Life, the road we're traveling, the mountain we're climbing, the game we play. The Trifecta surrounds it. It follows you like an aura. The further out of balance the Trifecta goes, the more at risk for suicide and disease you become.

We just took these two mental journeys to illustrate the polarity between perfectly balanced and perfectly broken.

The key to combating these disproportionate threats is simple.

It just takes a lot of hard work.

Balance is the ultimate goal and getting there mitigates suicide and disease. These are the two biggest threats for most of us, and many people skirt that edge, carrying massive mental weight throughout their lives. Unaware of how close to it they truly are.

It's not the equal division of the time itself. Balance is the harmonious division of your time between the Trifecta. You need to play with the cords until they align, creating a beautiful and unmistakable harmony. However, if you are to achieve balance, you need to understand something that took me many years to figure out.

Life is a mountain of pain and struggle designed to define us, but one of those "**F**" words is not like the others.

We can't change the landscape, so the mountain will stay, but we can change the trifecta to a dynamic duo.

You see, our family is the last thing we ever want to remove from this equation of balance. It has to stay. Otherwise, what's the real point of any of this? Also, fitness has to be maintained, right? If we turn it off, we accelerate our decay, and that's not optimal, so fitness stays.

Finances are a little different.

With finances, we can build a reserve and establish some alternative power sources. Family and fitness need ongoing management. There's no way to automate them, there's no magic pill, and there's no way around the work. They will always need active attention.

Finances, however, can be put entirely on autopilot. If it's on autopilot, it means you can virtually set it and forget it. That is the one essential thing I wish I would have had the vision to understand at a much younger age. It would have saved me years of struggle and negative stress, and here's why . . .

. . . It's a lot easier to carry two buckets up a mountain than three when you've only two hands and no help.

You can't just take two to the top, leave them, and come back for the third. Remember, the Trifecta is an aura. It follows you.

If you go up, it goes up.

If you go down, it goes down too.

It would be best if you found a way to get that financial bucket up the mountain without carrying it, but how?

CONNECTING THE FINANCIAL DOTS

Automating and transitioning from active income to passive income is how you do it. Active income is working for hourly or salary-based pay. It's limited and throttled. The moment you stop working, you stop getting paid, and we already know that can't happen, or the weight of your financial bucket will drop below the threshold and throw you out of balance.

Unfortunately, the longer you subdue yourself to active income, the longer it's going to take you to achieve this balance you crave. There's nothing wrong with earning an active style of income, so long as you don't depend on it to make ends meet. That's when the problems arise. When you rely on it and get taken out of the game for some unforeseeable circumstances, it forces you to hop on that roller coaster.

Remember, if you're like most people, you have less than $600 in the bank. That's not even enough to cover most mortgages or rent payments. So really, you're just broke. It's wise and feels great to have some savings, but savings will eventually run out. You can be frugal, sure, but most people are far from it, and they quickly find themselves in the front seat of that roller coaster.

It's better to have and make investments into things that give you a return with minimal work. It's better to have some passive income that flows in when you're unable to work. Enough passive income that it allows you the freedom to not have to get on that roller coaster of suffering.

Don't get passive income confused, though. Building a passive income will take more work than active income in all reality, but keeping it usually doesn't demand a lot. That's the difference.

Once you build the machines that power your passive income streams and automate a few things, you can begin to relax a little. You won't get paid while relaxing with an active income, but you will with passive income.

There's no real rest during the building of the machine, though. You'd be wise to solidify that understanding right now. At least if you want to get there with any life left to live.

What's with all this talk about mindset, finances, and career, though? This book is about survival and preparedness, after all.

What's the relevance?

Well, remember back when I asked myself . . .

. . . *"How can I cure suicide?"* . . .

I had determined that suicide and diseases are the disproportionate threats we should focus our preparedness efforts on first.

Well, I eventually concluded that financial uncertainty, more often than fitness or family stress, was responsible for most of the Trifecta's instability. When it all boiled down, financial issues were commonly at the core of most problems in my own life. It was also evident in many other lives that I examined during my years developing this method.

So, I had it! I dialed it in. I finally knew how I was going to attack the problem. I finally had my vector. The *"gray area"* started filling with *color.*

People kill themselves for all sorts of reasons, but from my perspective and analyses, many of those reasons appear to be subsets—byproducts of more significant underlying issues.

When you have a multi-tiered structure of symptoms and causes, it's vital to get to the root of it all if possible. Now, I'm not going to say that financial stress is THE root cause, but it's absolutely, from my observations, the one that sticks out the most and is typically not as difficult to overcome as many people make it out to be.

They just get lost in the fallacy of balance, trying to understand it due to the roller coaster effect.

Mental illnesses like depression, or substance abuse, and relationship problems are considered significant factors for suicide, but really, they are typically the byproducts of financial instability. There are, of course, exceptions to this just as there are with most things.

It's usually the finances that shake things up and cause problems in other areas of life. Not always, but a good majority of the time.

Money is not everything, but think about it like this . . .

How many people do you know that genuinely desire to be addicted to drugs or alcohol deep down? Probably none. Maybe it seems that way on the surface, but it's not what's at their core. I know I've never personally met a single addict past or present that wished to be so. It's usually just a coping mechanism for pain that grows out of control.

It was a last resort because they were ignorant of the path to take and didn't know where or what else to turn to. It's a poison band-aid, but this isn't always the situation. There are instances of ordinary people getting addicted through experimenting with these things as a form of fun. Stupid, nonetheless, but it happens. Either way the addiction develops, it's usually not intentional because we know that there's a high likelihood that it could kill us.

We are speaking specifically to drugs and alcohol, that is.

If we are to die from an addiction that brings joy and happiness into our lives, most of us would probably be at peace with it. If not, we will tone it down.

If I don't die in a bed by growing old, I hope it's by doing something I enjoy with the people I love.

Besides that, how many arguments do you get into that don't stem from finances? If you're anything like most people I've met and me, it's probably about 90% money motivated.

Divide the remaining 10% between general disagreements and "What's for dinner?" As we all know, that is the ultimate question in life, Haha! If you can solve that one right there, you'll be a wealthy individual.

Other than that, the only real relationship problems you'll typically see are infidelity related. However, If you have a faithful relationship, the main issues you will likely face will be financially motivated.

My perspective is that people don't choose suicide because they do not want to live, but because they want to end their suffering. They would gladly accept life if they knew how to stop it or lessen it to their manageable weight range.

That's what it comes down to, mitigation because suffering will always be part of the game in some capacity.

The relationship is rocky, so they turn to alcohol to numb it. The career sucks and doesn't pay enough, so they use hard drugs to escape it. PTSD's rough, and society doesn't provide proper support channels to combat it, so drinking and getting high become the low hanging fruit of relief when the system fails to help them fight back.

If those things scare you, maybe you do less life-threatening things to an addictive level as a way to escape. Such as gaming, or more relevant to this book, prepping. My point is, people will find a way to avoid suffering rather than face it. The problem is that it's always going to be there when you come back. Duct tape is, unfortunately, not a sustainable solution.

We have to repair the foundational cracks or rebuild them entirely. It's all weight on the bar, it all sucks, and if you don't stop it from accumulating, it will eventually fucking crush you.

You can only escape, cope, and stress so long before it starts to invite suicidal thoughts. Once you're at your max weight limit, you have a choice to make. Is it going to be suicide or self-awareness?

That's how rock bottom works, my friend.

Hitting it will either propel you upward like a trampoline with a new perspective or bury you into your grave.

The choice is yours.

However, we can consistently trace the vast majority of things that lead to suicide back to the financial sector of this Trifecta of Balance.

THE DIRECTION BECAME CRYSTAL CLEAR

At this point, it became evident to me that if I could help eliminate this one singular issue for people, I would be able to save and impact more lives positively and productively at scale. Way more effectively than if we were to focus on primitive skills or self-defense alone.

This is why a survival and preparedness book is heavily front-loaded with mindset concepts, relationship dynamics, financial talk, and general life lessons. It's why foundations are the first layer of the method and the largest percentage of the pie.

None of this preparedness stuff matters if you contemplate killing yourself or, worse, follow through with it.

So, let's continue with a couple more mental journeys.

Let's go back into visualization mode, shall we?

Let's use the same analogy as before—the perfect life vs. the perfectly shitty life. I want to explain to you what this roller coaster truly is.

The roller coaster is just merely another variation of the mountain of life. I wanted to give you multiple ways to view this whole concept of balance so that you truly understand how you can achieve it and keep it.

You can't effectively climb the mountain with all three buckets, and you can't truly get off the roller coaster without removing that financial bucket from the equation.

So, Imagine with me again.

You're doing great, life is excellent, and you got it all. Virtually perfect again. Feel it, smell it, see it, believe it.

Close your eyes and visualize this for a moment now.

Let's say this time; perfection is a tad bit more realistic looking.

This time, you work a job that you don't hate, but you can tolerate, and it pays you decently, but at the end of the day, you're still like most people and have less than a thousand dollars in the bank. You've achieved a slight glimpse of balance in life, but it's on thin ice. This is about as close to balance as most people manage to get, and it rarely lasts long.

You got the health, the family, and stable finances, but it's not secure. One hard blow and it's going to cause severe financial damage, and what do you know, here comes life, gloved up and ready to rumble.

Prepare for that first dip on the roller coaster.

Life decides that it's going to hit you with a blow to your transmission while you're on your way to work one morning.

You don't have enough money to fix this problem right now, so you have two options. You can work more or borrow it. If you're like most people, you've probably borrowed it more times than you can count already, and your friends, family, and banks refuse to lend to you anymore.

You're left with one option.

You have to work more hours because you haven't built any passive income streams, as we talked about earlier. You work active hours, and now you need more of them, but where will that time be sourced? It has to come from somewhere.

If you remember, I also told you earlier that we typically have 16 hours a day (the other eight devoted to sleep). We're primarily going to divide it between family, fitness, and finances to achieve this feeling of balance.

So, where are you going to get this extra time? Which "**F**" word are you willing to sacrifice time from to expand financially and recoup from this blow. . . Family or Fitness?

Most people are going to pick *Fitness*.

The family usually is always the last thing we like to sacrifice time from.

You're in maintenance mode, though, so you're not putting in absurd time in the gym and kitchen. You're where you want to be, so maintaining doesn't take as much time as actively trying to gain or lose weight.

So, you trade fitness for finances. Thankfully, you get a bunch of overtime at your current job, and you take on a second job with the remaining time you have. You need all the work hours you can get.

Now again, if you're like most people, it's probably going to take you about six months to save up enough money from those extra hours to justify such a significant expense because life's going to keep hitting you in the meantime. There's going to be other unforeseen expenses along the way, which prolongs the process of saving.

Six months pass by and thank God you earned enough money to get your transmission fixed.

Awesome job! Now you can get back to balance, right?

You scale back all those hours, quit the second job, and get back to "normal" work hours. The problem now is that you're not in maintenance mode anymore with your fitness. Six months of added weight and stress caused you to eat lots of fast food and occasionally drink to cope.

After six months of no gym and a dirty diet, you're starting to look a little hefty.

Let's call it thirty-five pounds overweight.

If you're like most, it will probably take you about another six months to burn thirty-five pounds of fat because, you know, life is going to keep hitting us. It's going to keep knocking us off the wagon, so it will take some time, but as you now know, that time has to come from somewhere.

Where's it going to be this time?

You need extra time because now it's no longer about maintenance. Now you have weight to lose and gains to get. Which demands more time than before for workouts and meal prep, so where are you going to get it?

It can't come from finances.

You already know we can't take time from there; otherwise, everything else falls apart. We wouldn't be able to feed ourselves or our family. We would lose the house, the cars, everything if we stop working. So, sacrificing from the financial sector isn't an option.

You know what that means, it has to come from family.

We never want to sacrifice time from our family, but at the end of the day, as much as it might suck, we can do it, and we will survive.

So, continue visualizing with me.

You commit to a new fitness regimen that demands more of your time. The family understands, though. They know you're doing this for them.

They know you're trying to stay healthy and in shape to live and provide for them long term.

They get it, for now. . .

In six months, the story might change.

Weeks go by, and you get the gains. Months go by, and you drop the weight. You take some more hits from life; you fall off the wagon cause you had to work some overtime, which slowed your progress down, but thankfully you didn't take any major blows, and six months have now passed, and you're finally back in shape.

You're finally back to where you feel in tune. Now you can go back into maintenance mode and spread those extra hours around into the family, and thank God because they were getting sick of your shit. You haven't been on a date or had a family night out in six months. On top of that, they question your loyalty since you're always gone or at the gym.

This is typically how it all consistently unfolds from my observations over the years.

I hear this story from my students and tribe members all the time.

Nonetheless, you're now back in harmony.

You have balance within your Trifecta of "**F**" words again.

It feels great for a brief moment, but you must remember that the financial sector will always be at risk until you build massive savings or replace it with a passive income strategy.

Saving your way to success is a very traditional and small-minded approach. It's also not very practical unless you put that money in the right place to gain interest at a higher rate than inflation. It's honestly probably the slowest and last method I'd ever recommend.

We won't go down that rabbit hole, though.

It just never works out like people think it will work because life will continue to fight you, and you're going to continue to take big shots. Anything you "Save" will get stolen away. You need to send your money soldiers to battle and let them bring back some prisoners if you catch my drift.

I am all for saving a few bricks of cash to go on the offense and chase a dream, but saving money for 20-30 years in hopes that you'll have enough to live a happy, easygoing life in the fourth and final quarter of the game is just a bad strategy.

Most of society isn't making enough to save enough for it to matter.

So what if you can save $200 a month? You're going to have to replace your tires; your heat pump will explode, your dog will need surgery, etc. Unforeseen circumstances always find a way to siphon your savings account.

This is why we see so many people saving and saving only to still be broke every year. It sounds logical on the surface. Just keep a little here and there, and over time you will have a bunch of money saved. It just doesn't typically work out that way.

You have to take some risks and embrace some struggle intentionally a few times in life. It truly is a requirement if you ever want off this awful roller coaster.

If you stay inside the "safe zone," life is going to find more ways to fuck with you. It's always going to find a way, but you can take many of those options off the table if you play the game right. If you want off this roller coaster, if you want to make it to the summit, if you wish to stop living in shit city, you have to understand all of these dynamics of balance.

I define success in a pretty straightforward way, but you'll frequently hear people trying to twist, turn, and construe the meaning to justify lackluster outcomes in their own lives. Way too often, you'll get advice from people who have failed and settled at damn near everything.

They say things like, *"Well, money doesn't buy happiness,"* or *"I don't need a bunch of money or a ripped body to be successful."*

They're not totally wrong, but the truth is almost always that they failed to achieve the money, the body, or the relationship, so they changed their definition of success to feel better.

Money doesn't buy happiness; you're right. Money does buy time, though, and you know what you can do with that time?

Things that make you fucking happy.

Having a ripped body won't determine your ability to succeed financially or live nice, but it certainly helps, and you know what else it gives you? More years on earth, mental clarity, and peace of mind. How about that? Think that might make you happy?

. . . *"Train insane or remain the same."* . . .

You may have heard that line a time or two.

We have to stop this widespread bending of the definition of success to help us feel better, especially when we choose to remain the same.

I've always spoken against the idea that we should learn to love ourselves and be happy with who we are, even when we're not who we want to be. It's a nice gesture, but it's not all that inspirational.

This framework doesn't breed progress. It breeds complacency and bad results. Today's society wants us to just fucking pretend it doesn't affect us.

It wants us to act as if that mental weight isn't causing massive amounts of stress that, over time, causes us to justify inaction and bad results. It provokes us to change the definition of success. It accelerates thousands of people closer to suicide day by day because they want us to pretend we're not under assault by the enemy.

There's only so long you can live that way, and If you continuously tell yourself it's okay to be broken, you'll stop trying to fix yourself. It's not okay to be okay with it.

We need to be real with who we are to define the actions we need to take to become who we want to be. Love yourself, and try to be happy, but make damn sure you frame it all in a way that keeps you on your toes. Complacency kills.

Being accepting and okay with who you are is only okay if you are who you wish to be. If you're not there yet, and you tell yourself every day that it's okay that you're not, you'll stop taking actions you know you need to be taking. You'll just become another sheep in the herd.

Eventually, you need to say enough's enough and flip your switch. I just hope that you have that moment now vs. later. Waiting until rock bottom, waiting until that max weight limit, is never something you want. Trust me; I've been through it.

You have to look yourself dead in the eyes and be real with yourself. You have to embrace some honesty for a change. The hardest thing for us humans to do is tell the truth... to ourselves. If you can keep it real with yourself, it's quite fascinating what you can do.

If you can't, you'll climb the mountain and ride the roller coaster your entire life. You will never obtain the balance you crave.

Self-awareness is the golden key to it all.

Perspective is everything, my friend. Bad situations and struggles can look like great opportunities with the right view. You can have an attitude that empowers or one that enslaves.

The easiest way to determine if you're on the right path is to look at your results. If your results aren't what you wanted, but you're taking all the action you can; it's your perspective that needs to be repositioned because you're making the wrong moves. You need to generate your action plans from the right mindset.

I hope that by understanding everything in this book, you can develop this new "Primal" perspective because I genuinely believe it will show you a clear path to the balance and proper preparedness you seek in life.

Besides creating life, there's really no greater fulfillment I've found than helping others find fulfillment in their life. This is what I sincerely hope I can help you accomplish in time.

We will talk more on the perspective shift towards the end, though, for now, let's cross a bridge.

PRIMAL'S WAR JOURNAL

DATE: FEB. 14TH 2015
SUBJECT: STAYING IN FOCUS

What you focus on expands. It truly is that simple. You must start paying closer attention to every word you speak, write, and think about.

It's all conditioning you to act and feel specific ways. If the reality you're experiencing isn't the one you'd like to see, it's because you're not in focus on the right things.

You have to be focused on what you want, not what you wish wasn't happening to you. Keep your focus locked onto the wrong subject, and you're bound to end up with a shitty picture.

That's not a product of circumstance, it's a product of focus—nothing more, nothing less. Focus is the key to achieving the things you want.

Good and bad things happen, and there's not a fucking thing you can do to control that. The only thing you can do is control the subject you're focusing on.

SECTION III: TRANSLATING KNOWLEDGE TO SKILL

CHAPTER 7

The Bridge

Connecting the dots between points A and B to develop life-saving and enhancing skill sets.

Now, I want to talk to you about the bridge between knowledge and skill. Some like to believe they are one in the same thing. That this bridge doesn't exist, but I assure you it's authentic.

An abstract idea of how something's done won't save you when your life's on the line. Get all the knowledge you can get; build the biggest mental library that you can. Just remember, if you don't reinforce your knowledge with actual experience, an abstract idea is all you're ever really going to have, and it just won't cut it.

I say this because of the variables, such as wind, rain, snow, cold, stress, or adrenaline. The brain and body respond differently when under the influence of these things. They make you forget what you thought you knew well. They cause you to drop the ball just when you think you've got a grip on it.

"The most important skill for survival is _____?"

I continue to see this question asked throughout time, and almost every time, the majority answer is the same.

. . . "**KNOWLEDGE!**" most will chant.

It's vital to remember that knowledge and skill are not the same and that you must bridge the gap between the two to develop the skill sets.

Knowledge is just knowledge.

Skill is the actual *repeatable and consistent application of that knowledge under stress and variable conditions*.

You might have some knowledge, but you don't have skill until you've experienced it. Only then will you have well-rounded awareness and know where you stand in performing a task.

Make sense? I hope so.

Let's venture into the void.

CHAPTER 8

The Void

Creating a solution to the pre-programmed emptiness. If growth and balance are what you seek, you must fill the dead space.

So, how do we fix the problem? How do we bridge the gap? It's quite simple, honestly... You train. You train hard, frequently, and intentionally introduce real-world variables into the equation to get you as ready for the real thing as you can be.

This concept applies to every aspect of life. We're not exclusively speaking to preparedness and survival skills here. We're talking about all life skills in general. However, I want to reinforce how critical it is that you understand how big of a deal bridging this gap truly is when it comes to skills related to your survivability.

Those skill sets should be a priority for all of us, yet somehow they tend to be placed on the back burner. Most people only train things they think are fun, and they only typically do so when it's convenient. In other words, a lot of people treat preparedness as a hobby rather than the priority that it should be, and it's much more than friction fires and primitive shelters.

We're talking total life preparedness because, once again, none of that cool and fun shit fucking matters if you're broken at the core.

Day after day, we all continue to standby and witness people trying to escape their lives because they lack the necessary skills to progress.

They read some books, listen to the gurus, and year after year, they fail to bridge this gap between knowledge and skill, yet wonder why they stay stuck.

My friend, you have to cross the bridge.

YOU HAVE TO FILL THE VOID

You have to execute it.

You must take action, and one of the solutions I have created to aid you within our organization is a gamified, incentivized, challenge oriented training process.

You see, naturally, there's this void that we all need to fill to see real growth in our lives. There's a lot of critical elements for growth that are just missing in most people's lives. Such as accountability, camaraderie, community, objectives, opportunities, and challenge.

They are certainly out there; most people just don't take advantage of them, but there's just not many effective options even for those who do. This was one of the driving forces behind why I created this entire operation and method. I figured I couldn't possibly be the only person out there experiencing this void in my life who can't find a good solution to fill it.

One thing I learned in the military is how powerful and beneficial camaraderie can be. True friendship brings a high degree of accountability to the table. Real friends care if you're progressing in the right direction, and they will help you stay that course. Unfortunately, thanks to social media, quality camaraderie is harder to find because real friends are harder to see. It's difficult to tell who's genuine or not when it's so easy to build a facade online. For so many, it's all about vanity. Everyone wants to look perfect, and in the online world, it's pretty easy to make people believe it.

SHARE THE LOWLIGHT REEL

Social media has become the place where we share the highlight reel of our lives. Everyone wants to share the highlights because the lowlight moments don't tend to feel too great, but I think there's a transcendent power in sharing them if you have the right perspective about it.

People already want to laugh at you when you fail. Hell, Fail Army built an entire business around putting people's failure out there for the world's enjoyment.

Failure is entertaining to the masses, and if you can learn how to laugh at yourself and grow instead of letting it bruise your ego, you will be much better off.

Not all failure is funny; sometimes, it's a severe issue. Such as failing to stay focused on nutrition over the holidays or failing to get that job you desperately need. Some things are just not amusing, unlike someone face-planting off a skateboard ramp. Funny failure should always be shared. I mean, why not? And it's easy to share it most of the time.

Serious failure always hurts to share, but I think it's beneficial to the growth and development of our skills and mindset that we do so. Not to promote the acceptance of it, or to encourage negative things, or anything like that. Share it to bring the pain of that failure to the front of your brain in the most impactful way.

The one thing that's worse than the failure itself is if someone else knows about it. Accountability is best when it comes from within, but most people lack the discipline to be consistent.

I like external accountability.

Someone other than ourselves.

If we are the only one who knows about a failure we have, it is easier for us to sweep it under the rug. This is why I am a massive advocate for outside accountability and transparency.

You need to develop your discipline and self-accountability, for sure, but to get you there, this can help. Don't knock transparency until you try it. If you don't have naturally high discipline, don't feel ashamed to ask for outside accountability.

It would be best if you confronted the pain this way because it's the one thing that's going to make you stay the course. It's what will help you get back on the wagon when you fall off. It's what will keep you focused for more extended periods.

Confront the pain, and share it to amplify it to the degree that makes you most uncomfortable. What do you do when you get uncomfortable? You move. And that, my friend, is when you'll grow and develop your skills. That's what real experience is.

You can't be afraid to share the "lowlight reel."

Our solution to skill development and bridging the gap is a massive database of missions/challenges you can partake in. As you complete them, the real reward is the development of skill. Still, because it's hard to get people to do anything (even things they enjoy), we incentivize participation with opportunities to win free gear, training, and more.

We also gamify the experience to introduce a healthy level of competition. Almost everyone loves to play games. The people who need this kind of training and lifestyle change the most tend to be obsessive gamers.

Trust me, I know, I was one, and I needed this desperately.

So I asked myself, *"Why can't we just turn life and preparedness into one big video game?"* I know some people already view life in this format but not in the way I envisioned.

They view it more like Pong, and I see it more like Zelda, or for you, young kids, Call of Duty versus Minecraft. The best way to play the game of life is to treat it like an adventure and not a competition. Let everyone else play Need For Speed while you play World of Warcraft. Gamification of your life through adventure, not competition alone. That's our solution, and it works phenomenally.

Take a step back and envision this with me at scale for a moment.

What if you could earn experience points for doing things you love then turn around and cash in those points for real tangible things? What if you could earn real money as well? Not just some sock money for the weekend, but some legitimate job-killing level money.

What if you could get experience points for things like taking your kids to the movies or your wife on a date night? What about building a primitive shelter, friction fire, or hitting the gun range?

What if you could make passive income by doing things like hunting, hiking, camping, bushcrafting, kayaking, fishing, lifting weights, training martial arts, and anything else you enjoy in the realm of preparedness?

That's the concept and intent behind the programs I have built inside of our Warrior Tribe. We want to provide you with the proper push and accountability you need to do the things you know you need to be doing more consistently. Not merely the stuff you want to be doing. Not only to build valuable skills but also to earn a living in a fulfilling way that you have loads of passion for.

Participating in our process shows us you are doing the work, and if you do the work, you will gain the skills.

Through this method, you will also get feedback from myself and other members to correct any issues and improve your skills even more.

Overall, this process provides a plethora of benefits. Mission by mission, we help you become more prepared mentally, physically, and beyond. Our missions range between fitness, mindset, survival skills, and much more. This process allows us to significantly impact people's lives at the skill level despite where they live.

It's all about getting hands-on, and I didn't want to confine myself to a classroom of people alone. I wanted a way to help people gain valuable skill sets regardless of where they live or their time zone.

It's easy to supply knowledge to anyone anywhere so long as they have access to the internet. Helping people develop skills from afar is a challenge, but we have built a strategy that's pretty damn effective at doing it.

IDENTIFYING THE ISSUE

The lack of skill to general knowledge was the big flaw in the industry that I saw. It's one thing to know how to make a friction fire, primitive shelter, or how to shoot a gun. It's a whole different thing to perform and complete those tasks effectively under stress and variable conditions.

What do you need to do differently when your hands are cold and numb? What do you need to do differently when your fire building materials are wet? What types of materials work best for wet weather? What might you forget when explosions are going off and people are screaming at you?

These are the things that typically go unknown unless you put yourself in the situation. These are the questions that don't typically get uncovered until we experience the situations first hand. Knowing how to do something and being able to do it. That's the difference. Just because you watch a video online on how to do something doesn't mean you'll be able to do it when it counts.

The videos and articles never prepare you for the variables you may encounter. They might tell you about them, but only experiencing them for real, or at the very least simulating them during training, will prepare you.

So, at this point, you now know what the significant threats are. You also understand that solidifying your foundation needs to become a priority if you want to build actual preparedness. To accomplish this, you must bridge the gap between knowledge and skill.

My question to you is, are you ready to take action?

We'll see how serious you are at the end of this book.

I'll ask you this question again near the end, but now, let's continue on this journey of enlightenment.

PRIMAL'S WAR JOURNAL

DATE: MARCH. 9TH 2016
SUBJECT: FUNDAMENTAL ROADSIGNS

You spend so much energy focusing on attempts at innovation to the degree that it takes your eyes off the road, It blurs your vision. It clouds your judgment. The "billboards" on life's highway distract you from your destination because of this impairment.

Follow the GPS. The plan you designed. The guide you crafted to get you to this point of interest. Your destination. Innovation is exciting, but arriving is more vital for your life right now. You need to get there.

Follow the fundamental roadsigns. The signs that remind you to stay focused. To not get sidetracked by every abstract billboard. You know the signs. You can feel them in your bones, and yet you choose to ignore them because a chance to innovate invigorates your soul.

Arrive at your destination, and you'll have every opportunity to innovate, and this time, you will be truly free to do so.

SECTION IV: WHEN PASSION BECOMES PURPOSE

CHAPTER 9

Finding Your Purpose

*Over my life, I have been a man of many endeavors. I've explored many passions in pursuit of my purpose. However, just because we might be passionate about something doesn't mean it's also our purpose. Passions can come and go, whereas purpose usually tends to be longer term. **Passion is the what, and purpose is why**. So, do you want to know how I answered the question everyone, struggles with? (Say yes)*

"What is my purpose?"

Most people will tell you that you'll know it when you see it, and it will speak to you in levels of certainty like you've never experienced before. I do believe this to be a mostly true statement. However, I don't think that it means discovering purpose is something that happens by chance.

I think the idea that "you'll know when you know" can lead us to believe that finding meaning is a random, unpredictable event. I don't have faith in this ideology due to how difficult finding purpose seems to be for most people.

I think it's vital to question everything grossly perceived as difficult, and that's what I did. After all, what better way for the tyrants to suppress us than to convince us that purpose is too difficult to grasp. The last thing the elitists want is for you to become influential enough to remove them from their power. It's hard to become that successful without a purpose.

I don't know; it's just a theory.

Either way, I began to question.

I feel it's the smart and responsible thing to do. Is purpose genuinely unpredictable, or could it be planned? Do we stumble into it one day magically, or more believably, is it something we become over a long period? Anything worthwhile tends to take some time, right?

Things that take time tend to require patience and a big reason **why**. It takes stamina. I created my purpose by exploring my passions until one of them stuck long term. Not by waiting around, hoping it would just appear one day soon.

I figured if I got burnt out, there's no way it was my true calling. The thing is, you're going to experience burnout during any long term journey. There are always some aspects of the pursuit that you won't enjoy, which will lead to burnout. I concluded that it's not so much about what burns out but more about what's staying lit, and you need the right fuel to stay lit. If the passion stays lit long term and continuously grows year after year, you've likely begun the transformation from passion to purpose.

I love the part of my journey where I witness people transform their lives using things I've created. However, I'm not too fond of the parts with extremely long nights and years of suffering and sacrifice that it takes for me to experience those moments.

Suffering is a requirement, though, so I learned to see it as something that helps me rather than hurts me. The deciding factor between passion and purpose is whether or not you are getting the right fuel for the fire. The bigger your fire, the easier it is to tolerate the discomforts. That is how you overcome the inevitable burnout during the pursuit of long term goals—that, and setting yourself up with a solid plan with plenty of milestones.

We love checking boxes.

It makes us feel good about the work we're doing.

If we are frequently passing milestones and doing things that generate the right fuel, chances are, we are fulfilling our purpose.

It honestly doesn't have to be more complicated than that. Many things don't have to be as complicated as we make them out to be.

I believe purpose is one of them.

As I have said, many times, perspective matters. You will probably catch me saying this a few more times too. Yes, there is a certain nobility in solving complex problems, and I think we should all strive to ultimately address a few in our life. Still, I also believe that they bring an immense stress level into our lives that can easily be crippling if pursued at the wrong time.

I think mastering the simple things first will set you up for greater success in the long term. Ultimately, your purpose may turn out to be solving a complex problem for the whole world, but before you can do that efficiently, you must first solve a lot of simple issues for yourself. You know, crawl before you walk, walk before you run. It's all about the building blocks, my friend.

So, the next question became, **"What kind of fuel do I need?"** Simply enjoying something is not going to cut it. I analyzed for a while and discovered a common theme amongst the things I was successful with long term, something distinctly different.

The things that I burnt out on didn't significantly impact anyone's life in a meaningful or positive way. I'm not saying they couldn't have; I'm just saying they didn't at the time. Once more, perspective matters.

All the things I had success with long term had astronomical impacts. These impacts quickly turn into the most efficient form of fuel you can use—raving fans and their testimonials.

Trust me; nothing stokes your flames quite like being told your work is why someone is still breathing. When people attribute major life successes to you, it's honestly one of the world's best feelings. You will be incredibly proud, but always remember to be grateful and humble at the end of the day. Pride can prevent you from realizing your purpose if you're not careful.

So, that's it! The missing link, and the reason, I believe, so many people struggle to realize their purpose. I think the road to our true calling is paved with intentionality. It's not random. They say "you'll know it when you see it," but I believe **you have to see it, to know it.**

Simply put, I think that we are the architect. Purpose doesn't just appear; you create it, and to do that, you need to live in **action mode versus reaction mode**. It's a simple shift in perspective, but as it goes, the simple things have always proven to take a lot of discipline.

Why is it so damn hard for us to do the little things that would improve our lives? Ever wonder why that is?

I think it's the small monotonous things that truly move the needle for us in life. You see, I believe purpose is a relatively simple equation. We humans just have a way of science-ing the shit out of everything until it's too complex to understand.

On the surface, defining your purpose sounds like a complicated question, but it doesn't have to be. We are conditioned to believe that logically, complicated issues must have complicated solutions, right? Well, sometimes yes, but other times, no. Often, the most effective solutions have straightforward equations. Simplicity tends to prevail more often than not.

When we skip the simple things, we may not endure pain right off, but you best believe it will get excruciating if you ignore them for too long. The bigger, more complex things tend to carry more weight in terms of pain. We develop this idea that if we don't do them now and fast, the pain will be substantial and immediate.

This is why it's so much easier to buy a gym membership than to go to the gym or consistently eat healthy meals. Setting the goal is fun and far easier to do than the work required. Declaring it in front of the world gives us a massive hit of dopamine, making us feel like we are accomplishing something when we aren't. Buying that gym membership somehow makes us feel like we are getting in shape when, in reality, it's not doing a damn thing.

I prefer to talk about results, not so much my goals.

This is hard to do.

But remember, it's not setting the intention that excites you, but rather, the thought of fulfillment.

Our brain wants that dopamine, so it tells you to stake your claim to the world and unleash it. And it will, but when it fades, you will be no closer to the goal whatsoever. So it's best if you try to contain the goals.

It's much easier to talk about it than it is to be about it because to be, means to do, and doing great things that generate the right fuel means doing many small things consistently over a long period. This has proven to be a difficult challenge. The more we talk about what we plan to do, the less likely we are to do it.

Talking about the plan doesn't help you; it hurts you, even though it feels good when you do it. Instead, show and tell what you've done, or at the most, are actively doing—precisely, the results.

Doing it from this angle won't only give you more dopamine; it will provide you with enough to carry into future things to keep your momentum going versus take away from you. If the dopamine hit is coming by talking about results and not what you merely plan to do, it has nothing to take away.

This perspective will help you tremendously.

Dopamine must be kept in check. Too little and life gets incredibly dull, too much and you become destructively addicted, and too much of a good thing can be harmful.

I think it's vital to make yourself earn your dopamine. You have to do the work. It's confusing, I know. Dopamine is readily available all around us. It's like, this is what we all want and crave, and it's right here in front of us in unlimited supply, so why the fuck would we work for it?

Working for a dopamine boost when it's sitting for free right in front of us? Blasphemy! I promise you, though, you need to make yourself earn it.

It's essential to try and balance this so that you stay productive. If you're not right in the middle, your productivity is dipping in one way or another.

Are you playing games a lot? You're probably gaining weight.

Are you watching a ton of TV?

You're probably missing out on extra income opportunities.

Newton's third law. *"Every action creates an equal and opposite reaction."*

When you take massive amounts of action in one area, something else on the other side could be negatively affected. Your dopamine exposure can and needs to be balanced every step up the mountain, unlike the Fallacy of Balance within the Trifecta, which is really only possible at the apex.

So, you want to know what your purpose is, yeah?

The reason for which you exist?

Your ultimate goal?

Follow passions that generate that "raving fan" fuel. Eventually, one or a combination of those passions will become your purpose.

From that moment on, you will no longer have doubts about your heading.

My purpose didn't take shape until I thoroughly explored about twelve different business ideas and failed (learned) a lot. Something you need to understand, though, is that purpose can evolve. You need to focus on simply being in alignment with it because it can and will change, kind of like Murphy's Law.

This is another big reason I believe it's something we create and become, versus happenstance.

I have my purpose now, but it's kind of like a living thing. It evolves, and when you fulfill one, you create another one, a bigger one. The truth is, it's impossible to know what your end-all-be-all mission is going to be. You just need to be aligned with it.

Let me explain . . .

See, growing up, I was heavily invested in sports.

I played basketball, football, soccer, and in my free time, I would skateboard. I loved sports so much that I thought it was destined to be my career. Then one day, while playing ball, a kid swept my legs while I was mid-air. I crashed hard and broke my arm for the fourth time in the same damn spot. It was a nasty compound fracture this time. Being this was my fourth time doing this, and how bad this break was, I had to have surgery.

I was a kid back then, so when the Dr. told me that I was close to them having to amputate it at the elbow, that shit scared me a little. My luck was terrible too. I mean, who breaks their arm four times in the same spot before making it to high school?

I took it as a sign.

From that day on, I stopped playing sports, skating, and virtually all things physical. To fill the void this decision created, I turned to gaming.

Now, when I have a real passion, I explore it relentlessly.

This means I didn't just play games after school. I played them competitively online; then, I started a team and created a gaming organization. I loved gaming so much that I thought it was destined to be my new, true career.

I did this quite a few more times coming up.

I loved designing and art, so I started a little graphics business.

I enjoyed the car scene, so I started a car club.

I ran a buy, sell, and trade store.

I became a real estate agent, joined the military, freelanced media & marketing services, and many other things. All of this and more before I was even old enough to buy a beer.

But I don't say any of this to boast.

Frankly, I don't even feel comfortable telling people I failed at so many things.

I'm just telling you because I like to practice what I preach about transparency and reinforce my point that *"just because we might be passionate about something doesn't mean it's also our purpose."*

As you were just informed, I have a lot of things I am passionate about. I was freakishly good at some of these things too. If I had had the right perspective back then, it's hard to say how different my life would look like today. I am very happy with where it led me, but not with how long it took me to figure it out. Life's short. It's important to seek knowledge and be open to different perspectives to shave the learning curve.

A few years after joining the military, I quit gaming for good. At least until I hit a particular goal. It had become an unhealthy addiction that wasn't paying the bills. I vowed never to play games again until I was wealthy, happy, and healthy. So, I got ready for the next endeavor, which ended up becoming the very conduit for the words you're reading now.

I did it. I finally found the missing link! I finally got it right. However, It wasn't until about 4-5 years into this adventure that I knew that. I knew I got it right because I could feel the differences in fuel.

You remember the fuel I mentioned, right?

I had finally found it.

I was routinely getting messages, emails, phone calls, and more from people across the globe, telling me that what I was doing was making significant positive impacts on their lives. I knew I had to be doing something right because the feedback and "fuel" I'm getting now feels different. Like it was meant to be versus being forced into existence.

I was performing better, felt genuinely happy, and checked off milestones daily. My fire was burning hotter, brighter, and bigger than ever. It kept growing year after year too. I knew I had finally found my purpose, and by found, I mean created it through massive action and exploration.

I wasn't lucky; I made it. I worked insanely hard at it.

I believe this is the real reason it takes most people a lifetime to figure out their purpose. They don't explore or take nearly enough action, which means fewer passions get pursued over a more extended period. It leaves many people stuck in the gray zone, and time isn't something we have a lot to spare.

DON'T GET STUCK IN THE GRAY ZONE

The gray zone is that area in the middle. Where you're not really living, you just kind of exist. Can you resonate with that feeling?

Have you ever felt like you were merely existing? Like you needed to get up and do something with your life? Like there's something huge that could be great, and you're missing out?

Lord knows I have.

I don't blame laziness entirely for so many people lacking purpose. I think it's more of a flaw in our beliefs about it and how we find it. If more people had the perspective that you can create your purpose, they would explore more and take massive action.

However, since we have mystified the shit out of this word *"Purpose,"* many people get lazy and buy into that *"you'll know it when you see it."* random event perspective.

Years go by, and they take less and less action. Routines become routine, and passions become things you would make time for, **BUT...**, you know, excuses. By this time, bills crush you into the ground, friends ignore you, family life is crazy, you have no time for anything, and even if you did, you would be too fucking exhausted to "explore" it.

Sound familiar at all?

When was the last time you did something you are passionate about with the same intensity you had growing up?

It's much harder to go exploring when you're an adult with a family and real-life problems. That's why I put so much pressure on young people to go all-in while having no pressing responsibilities. It's very challenging, but not impossible. It's not an option that's exclusive to younger people either.

You have to get your priorities straight. You need to ask yourself if you're here to exist or actually live. If you commit to living, you will create the time to explore passions and find your purpose. We make time for the things we genuinely care for the most, period. *"I don't have time for that."* is one of the most frequent lies I hear. I've helped a lot of people with their goals and time management. Typically, I find they have more than enough time for it.

So, to find that purpose, you must first make time to pursue some passions. As you're exploring them, listen carefully to the feedback. Not just any feedback, though. The two specific things I want you to listen to are the hard data and fuel. Nothing else matters.

CHAPTER 10

Hard Data & Fuel

*Dr. Suess said it best. "Be who **you** are and say what **you** feel because those who mind don't **matter**, and those who **matter** don't mind."*

Are you progressing well? Does the data tell you your growth is on the right track? If you're smashing goals and checking boxes frequently, great! Keep going. If not, maybe just keep this passion as a hobby, because it's probably not your purpose.

It doesn't matter how much you enjoy it. If you're not actually good at it, it's not going to be something that can create the right fuel. It's essential to make this decision fast because you will waste many years of your life chasing the wrong passion, and it will never lead to purpose.

It doesn't mean you can't enjoy the thing you love. It just means it's not your purpose. Of course, give yourself a reasonable amount of time and effort to gather enough data to make a sound decision. Don't stop when the first random hater tells you that you suck. Don't listen to negative opinions much at all.

Also, don't be naive and think every raving fan is telling you the truth. Sometimes raving fans are close friends and family who don't want to hurt your feelings, so they lie to you. You need to have a strategic filter when it comes to consuming all this feedback.

There are different types of feedback. There are people's opinions, and there's hard data. Only listen to hard data. If you want to get technical, I guess hard data is still ultimately the result of people's opinions, but people's opinions aren't always the result of hard data.

Most people who tell you that you suck at something didn't conclude that by looking at the data. They do this the same way the media hides the full story from us. We only see what they want us to see, and sometimes, that's not the truth.

Haters only see the surface. They're the people judging books by their covers rather than their substance. They thumb down your YouTube videos before even watching them.

Only pay attention to the data. A thumb down, lower sales, or 50% fewer engagements is much easier for you to digest and grow from than listening to a haters essay about how much you suck. Sometimes people are just jealous and bitter, and you need to ignore them. This kind of feedback is typically just a reflection of their shortcomings, and if you allow people to dump their sewage into your life, don't be surprised when it starts smelling like shit.

People and their opinions can prevent you from becoming the creator you need to be if you don't tune them out.

Understand the difference between hatred and constructive criticism from a fan, though. If you're reading a comment, message, or email, and the tone sounds negative or malicious, stop, block, and go back to work.

It's pretty easy to spot the difference. Real haters are typically pretty direct. Identify them, and tune them out. There will always be closet haters, but there's not much you can do about them until they out themselves. They usually like to disguise themselves as a friend, but you'll notice they only chime in to say, "*I told you so*" or "*you should have done it this way.*" They always have something "*clever*" to say. They like to argue during the weekdays and say, "*you go! Crush it.*" on the weekends. Once you get familiar with their ways, even closet haters become easy to identify. You have to cut them out of your life, no matter who they are.

As a creator, there's a fine line between feedback, fulfillment, and destruction. Without the right dynamics, it can ruin you. As a creator, it's fundamental to listen to feedback, but at the same time, it's equally important to not give a fuck. If you create purely based on others' expectations and desires, you're just facilitating the creations of someone else, not your own, and mentally that's the wrong place to be. It will burn you out very fast, and you'll grow to hate the hobbies you once enjoyed.

So which is it, *Ian*?

Do I need to care or not?

Do I listen to the damn feedback, or do I ignore it?

I know this all sounds slightly contradicting, but you need to do both, just in a strategic way.

Care and listen to some things, ignore others. *"Take everything with a grain of salt,"* as they say. My strategy is to listen to the people who care about listening to me, my supporters.

Anyone who genuinely cares about your feelings will at least try to frame their criticism constructively with a positive tone. Unless it's the fifteenth time and you're stubborn, haha.

People who harbor hatred for you don't care about your feelings and want you to suffer the same as they do.

It's important to ignore them entirely because what they have to say isn't evidence-based, it's purely emotional, and its sole intent is to convince you to stop. I said it once, and I'll repeat it, *"Don't stop when the first random hater tells you that you suck."*, or even the 131st, or 500th, for that matter.

As a creator, I have learned that it's vital to do what you want to do. Create what you want to create. I listen to data to determine if I'm half-decent at something or not to prevent me from wasting too much time with it if it's something I'm trying to turn into a career.

Passion is cool, but you need to truly be good at what you do if it's to become your purpose. I know my passion, but hard data tells me if I'm actually good or not. Beyond that, unless framed constructively, I don't give a single shit about feedback and opinions regarding my work. If the data tells me I'm good, I'm going to pursue it regardless of what any lone person says or thinks about it, and I think you should do the same.

Feedback can be a dangerously tyrannical thing if you don't get strategic about how you consume it. You can always get better at your craft, but sometimes you're flat out doing the wrong thing.

I'm naturally gifted at a lot of things. It's been a blessing and a curse. For a long time, it made me very skeptical. I was always questioning if I was on the right path or not. I didn't understand that it doesn't matter how much joy something brings me if it's not fueling the fire inside.

I have loved every passion I ever explored.

Every single one of them brought me enormous amounts of dopamine. However, not all of them generated the fuel I needed to stay lit. That's when I knew something wasn't my purpose, and I needed to move on.

My friend, if you plan to venture down the path of creation, please know this. Whether you create music, play games, make videos, write books, paint pictures, or put yourself out there in any way, shape, or form, you will be attacked.

You mustn't allow these attacks to compromise the entire reason why you wanted to create something in the first place.

Do you think all the *"it's so ugly!"* comments will stop Elon Musk from creating Cyber Trucks or launching rockets to space? What about Steve Jobs? Do you think he should have shelved the iPhone project when people chanted, *"but Android has had this for years!"*...?

How about Jeff Bezos. Do you believe he should have given up when people said, *"This will never work, you could never compete with Walmart."*...?

Donald Trump, when people negatively criticize him enough to make any average man want to off himself multiple times a day.

Do you think people who have accomplished great things in life pay attention to hatred?

David Goggins, when people tell him he's crazy. That *"Running a 250-mile race isn't safe or smart."*

"You should work smarter, not harder,"... they tell him.

What about Conor *"Notorious"* McGregor, Kevin Hart, or Will Smith? Do you think legends sit around and listen to the noise? Fuck no! They work.

They know It will prevent them from creating and pursuing their passions if they care deeply about what other people think of them or their work.

Listen to the data. That's the only feedback you need.

Opinions, not so much...

Good data only promises that you're doing something you're good at, not that it's your purpose. It's undoubtedly a good indicator that it might be, but what cements it is whether you're getting the right fuel.

Remember, I said there are two types of feedback you should pay attention to, *"**hard data and fuel.**"*

You generate this fuel by doing something that substantially impacts people's lives in a positive way. It goes much deeper than likes, comments, and shares. It's what confirms to you that you are in tune with your current purpose.

If the analytics look good, and you're hitting milestones, you know the passion has **potential**. If your fire continues to grow and you get the fuel you need to stay lit, you know the passion has a **purpose**.

One thing to bear in mind is that sometimes a passion turned into a profitable business is just a conduit for you to do something even more significant.

Maybe this awesome thing you love and are successful with will eventually enlighten you to something more. You would never know it until you go through it and find out, though. It doesn't mean that what you were doing wasn't your real purpose, it was, but you can fulfill a purpose.

There are levels to it.

Don't think less of yourself if your passion doesn't turn into a world-changing mission. Not everyone has the same capacity for greatness, and that's okay. We're all instruments of God, and we all sound unique.

People get this idea that their goals aren't worthy enough unless they include becoming a superhero and saving the world. This is just a toxic way to think, and it holds so many people back from seeing what they're truly made of. Not everyone has the same ambition. It's okay if you can't become a superhero, haha!

Knowing your purpose isn't exclusive to people with mega ambition. However, ambition can grow. If you want to be more ambitious, surround yourself with ambitious people. It will naturally help you grow.

I'm not telling you to be okay with setting the bar lower.

Never do that.

I'm just telling you to be okay with the size of your purpose that you feel it is now.

Don't lose interest, slow down, or quit because you feel like it's not grand enough. Just keep doing what you're doing, and surround yourself with better, more ambitious people, and it just might become something bigger than you can imagine. Remember, you create this purpose through action. It's not going to appear suddenly. You must keep pursuing the passion if you want it to come into focus fully.

So, a long-ass story long... Make the time, explore your passions, check some boxes, listen to the hard data, and make sure you are getting the right fuel.

I wanted to talk about my perspective on purpose in this book because I believe the lack of it to be a massive contributor to suicide. I also think it's a huge aspect of our foundation for growth as a human being and our overall preparedness.

Next, let's talk about what we are doing about all of these challenges. Such as obtaining balance, the facade, the weight limit, the disproportionate threats, getting to the root, the bridge, the void, etc. You know, the solutions.

PRIMAL'S WAR JOURNAL

DATE: JULY. 23RD 2018
SUBJECT: GOOD BAD TEMPTATIONS

During your mission, the prophecy you're truly called to fulfill. You will be tempted to stray from the objective by things that look and feel good that can ultimately lead to adverse outcomes. Outcomes that are so far from where and what you're supposed to be that it will paralyze you.

Not every temptation is a bad opportunity, but any opportunity that isn't in line with the mission takes you further away from accomplishing it. Never make a hasty decision when everything is on the line and you're under attack from temptations, despite how good the opportunity may appear...

You might need to give in to the temptation, though, it could be the best decision you ever make. Just heavily weigh any decision when it pertains to matters of your heart and soul. Make a smart choice, and remember to execute confidently. The temptations often feel good, but more often, they're just bad for business.

SECTION V: CREATING MORE SOLUTIONS

CHAPTER 11

Accountability

You already learned about some of the solutions we created to bridge the gap and fill the void regarding knowledge and skill development. The gamification of life and training turned out to be an incredibly effective tactic to get people doing the work to improve their lives and prepare them. It helps you do the things you don't necessarily want to do but know you need to. The next step is to implement some accountability measures to ensure you stick to it long term.

Our tribe is the combination of many different systems collectively working together to solve all of these challenges. As I already covered earlier, people grossly lack accountability, so the next solution we created was an accountability program that we call **W.A.S.P.**

(Warrior Accountability & Strategy Partner). We designed it to help people stay consistent over more extended periods.

With this program, we pair you with another member and give you strategic tasks to accomplish together geared towards total life preparedness. Not only will you communicate and work with your partner, but you will also do the same with our certified coaches on an ongoing basis.

It will help you develop your discipline and keep you focused on the right objectives, both in the tribe and your life. As I said, The Primal Method focuses on total life preparedness, the big picture. Not just one or two small widgets. With us, it's not uncommon to build a friction fire in the morning, shoot firearms in the evening, and learn how to build a business or love your family better at night.

Preparedness is so much more than what we see on television shows. Some issues lie beneath the surface that are killing people, and I aim to do something about that. None of the fancy things mean much if you're not happy to live your life at the end of the day.

A fractured foundation cannot be fixed with duct tape, yet that's essentially what many people try to do. I can't even tell you how many *"prepared"* people I have directly worked with and observed over my years that are trying to escape a broken life through prepping.

Much like people drink and do drugs to escape the pains of reality, people also do other things they love that we don't consider harmful. Many people with a prepared mind tend to focus on the things they enjoy most, like fishing, hunting, guns, gear, or self-defense. They often do these things to escape the pains of a fractured foundation in the same way that others sometimes resort to drugs or alcohol.

Foundations aren't typically perceived as sexy and fun things to work on, so they get neglected. Our WASP program and Warrior Tribe aim to help you find growth and hold you accountable for it. Not only in all the areas of preparedness you love but also in the **critical foundations that support them**. Think of this program like the military's battle buddy system, only with a little more intentionality and accountability.

CHAPTER 12

Opportunity

You can see a challenge as an obstacle to overcome or an excuse to succumb to mediocrity. If there's a will, there's a way. Luckily for you, I have created the way. All you need is some will power. I got sick of hearing the excuse of "I can't afford it," so naturally, I created the solution that renders that excuse invalid: reasons or results, not both, my friend.

As time progressed and we evolved, the next big challenge I discovered was, you guessed it, financial. Not only is financial instability one of the leading causes of suicide, but it also directly affects your ability to live a prepared life.

You need money to buy gear, food, water, ammo, training, and everything else.

Instead of just being a community that you can pay to be a part of, *I wanted to create a community that could pay you to be a part of it*. So I decided to build an affiliate program. I dubbed this program, The Vanguard.

BE A WARRIOR, NOT A WORRIER

The Vanguard is the forefront of an advancing army. It's the group of people who lead the way in new ideas and developments. In short, it's our most active and supporting members who are acting as ambassadors for our mission.

When you join our tribe, you get access to this program. I didn't just want to create something capable of helping you earn a little gas money, though. I wanted this to be a genuine career opportunity. A way for you to monetize your passions with a low barrier to entry. A way to help you kill your dreadful *"Job"* and replace it with something you actually enjoy.

I had this idea in my head...

What if I could help people get paid to become prepared? To get paid to do the things they love to do concerning preparedness.

Like practicing bushcraft, training mixed martial arts, shooting guns, hiking, camping, hunting, fishing, etc.

This all sounds far fetched, right?

Get paid to do what you love. I know it sounds crazy, but Steve Jobs said, *"it's the people who are crazy enough to think they can change the world that end up doing it."*

Now, you can certainly go right now, do what you love, and create or find a way to get paid for it. However, I have built something that hands you that opportunity on a silver platter. Creating and hunting for an opportunity takes a lot of energy. Please take my word for it. I have lived it. I wish I had been offered such a fantastic opportunity myself. I prefer the simplistic route.

Like I said earlier, simplicity prevails.

CHAPTER 13

Active Vs. Passive

Freedom is a lot closer than you think it is.

We briefly touched on active and passive income earlier, but I want to clarify it a little better for those of you who may not truly appreciate the latter's gravity.

When it comes to how you earn your money, there are two main ways to do it.

Actively or passively.

An active income refers to money earned for services rendered. This includes salaries, wages or tips, commissions, and any income that required material participation—a typical hands-on 9-5, for example.

Passive income is the opposite. It refers to income earned with virtually no involvement. In short, the more passive income you make, the more comfortable and better life can be.

The first goal is always to replace the amount of money you need to pay all of your bills. Many people think you need a lot of money stacked up to retire when all you need is enough passive income flowing in to cover your living expenses.

Also, when I say the word *"retire,"* I mean a transition to a life with more freedom of choice to do what you love to do.

Think about it.

If you have $2,000 in bills a month, all you need to effectively *"retire"* is $2,000 in passive income every month. Not millions of dollars in the bank. You just need enough to pay your bills on autopilot. Once you achieve this, you will have the freedom of choice to earn and live; however, you see fit for the most part.

You can still shoot for millions, and you should. Only now you can do it the way you dream about, instead of slaving and saving to come up short in the end still.

If you already understand all this economic language about passive and active income, great. You're already a big leg up. Most people don't truly understand this and how important it is, though. Active income is all most people know. Sometimes for their entire life. Let's not even get into the fact that if you get hurt or sick and can't work for a long time, that all of your active income vanishes.

Passive income will be there whether you're sick, on vacation, taking a nap, or laid up with broken legs. Passive income is what you want and need. So, I created a passive income solution for you with a shallow entry barrier, lots of free training, and all the support you'll need.

Everything you need to succeed wrapped up in a beautiful box. We even put a bow on it to make it extra special, haha!

RAISING THE BAR

I decided that there was no other way for this program to be a real opportunity than to be equally generous to our members. To equally support those who support us. So, I decided to offer up to 50% recurring commissions.

This level of opportunity is scarce and almost unheard of when it comes to affiliate programs. With us, you can kill your job and get paid to become prepared, and I will personally be teaching you exactly how to do it.

I'm not interested in just helping you earn enough to pay a utility bill or car payment, though. Preparedness can become your career, and with us, that also means a happy life with solid foundations. All you have to do is join us and pick up what we put down.

The tribe does cost money to be a part of, but it pays for itself ridiculously easily, and potentially so much more if you want it to. I don't want to go into the nuts and bolts of this program in this book, though.

You will learn more about it when you become a member yourself. We want you to be a member first and an affiliate second. You must understand and live the lifestyle first and foremost if you're going to have real success as an affiliate. Just know that the Vanguard program can and will unlock some significant doorways for you if you participate.

These programs and systems I've mentioned are just a tiny fraction of the total package. There are so many other resources we have to help you. Like life planning tools, bill management tools, opportunities for work, discounts to gear companies, communication tools, events, preparedness training, and so much more.

There are other perks that weren't even intentional too. Byproducts that occur when you live the way we live. Like curing depression or combating PTSD.

The tribe evolves like most things, and it continues to do so every day. I will be building valuable resources until the day I die.

I could write an entire book on the benefits alone, but I'm honestly not trying to hard-sell you on anything other than the Primal Method itself here. Because regardless if you wage war alone, with us, or with anyone else, you can take these concepts and apply them to your life and preparedness.

That's the beauty of it.

Yes, our tribe will dramatically help you enhance it all, but it's not a requirement to apply the method. I think after you finish this book, you will quickly see how joining us could be the best decision you'll ever make. In fact, I know it would be. The only thing I can't be sure of is how committed you are to real preparedness.

I'll leave it to you to explore the rest of our many facets and solutions to enhance your life.

PRIMAL'S WAR JOURNAL

DATE: JAN. 17TH 2020
SUBJECT: PEACE & VANITY

Instead of wishing for the impossible, find comfort in the fact that they could never truly understand your sacrifices.

Let it go.

All the moments, creations, thoughts, and things you experience along the path will never truly be fully known or understood by anyone but you.

You must be at peace with this fact if you want peace in life.

They will ultimately never understand it the way you do, no matter how it's framed. **Let go of vanity.** Detach yourself from the bondage of other people's perceptions. That's the only way to be free and at **peace** with who you are, and the adventures you've yet to embark on.

SECTION VI: THE LAYERS

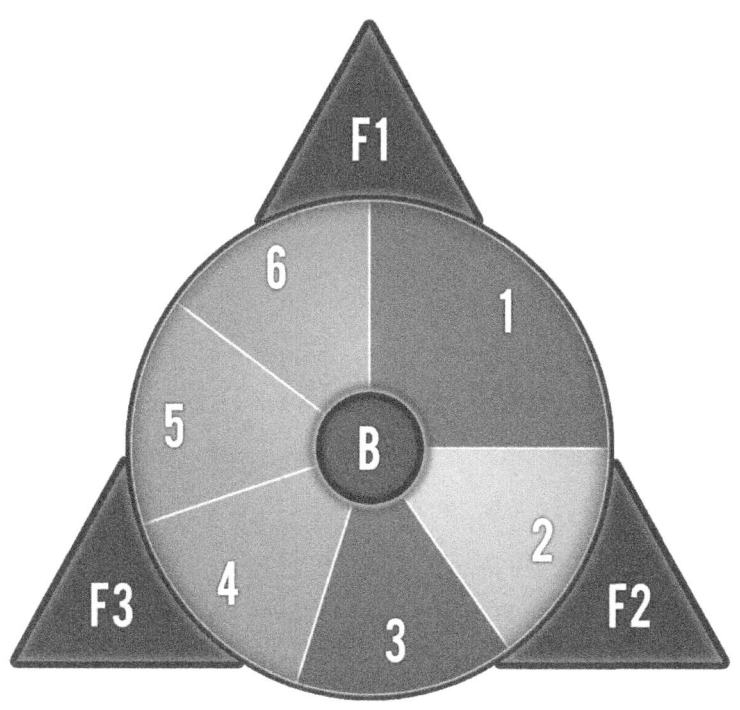

Layer 1 - Foundations

Layer 2 - Health & Fitness

Layer 3 - Unarmed Combatives

Layer 4 - Armed Combatives

Layer 5 - Prepping

Layer 6 - Operational Skills

CHAPTER 14

The Inception

*Right now, you probably wish I'd have begun this whole journey here. However, I needed to ensure you understood the **why** before the **what**. It's only partly beneficial to know what the method is. If you want optimal performance, you need to understand why it is as well, and I figured if I put this in the beginning, most people would read about the layers of the method and not pay attention to the rest of the book. You must understand both sides of this process if you genuinely want it to work for you in all aspects. So, I told you the reasons why it works. **Now, we can dive into what it is.***

For the longest time, there was that gray area in my life. A zone that seemed impossible to define, and it drove me crazy at times.

I thought I knew my purpose.

I knew why it was and what it was; I just didn't know **how** it would become a reality. I couldn't describe the process of getting there.

I didn't entirely understand how I was supposed to get from point A to point B. So, I figured if I just kept taking action in one way or another, the blueprint would eventually reveal its full self, and that's exactly what happened.

One night, after years of massive action, it finally came into focus for me. God planted the seeds in the beginning, and he finally came back around to water them. Shortly after, the concepts grew like bamboo in my mind. This is how it genuinely felt.

I had an epiphany, and the Primal Method was born.

Will it ultimately be as grand as I feel it is?

Time will tell...

All I know is that I believe God put these ideas in my head to save and change lives in significant ways, and I don't want to waste or disrespect that gift.

THE EXACT MOMENT IT HAPPENED

I was somewhere around 30 minutes into an ice-cold shower one night. I am a big fan of Wim Hof and his methods of using cold exposure and breathwork to overcome many obstacles in life. I take cold showers and do breathwork virtually every day.

Cold exposure can do many great things for you, but my favorite benefit has to be the levels of clarity and focus it forces me to have. When you submerge yourself in ice water, your brain and body go haywire. It removes all thoughts and forces you to focus on your breathing.

As you get things under control and your mind gets a little more freedom, all your thoughts will start stacking back up.

In the beginning, though, it will be slow. Think of it as an ice block. You "froze" yourself, and you have to thaw out. This takes a little time, which means your thought floodgates aren't just blowing apart and coming right back to overwhelm you. This gives you time to think clearly and process the thoughts more thoroughly as they slowly flow back in.

Realizing this, I decided to use it strategically, and I tried to make the first thoughts that flowed back revolved around defining this gray area. I needed to focus on them clearly, and there's no better time to do this than deep into a numbingly cold shower. There are just too many thoughts to process at any other time during the day, and turning them off on command is not a simple task.

So, I got intentional. I even wrote my questions on a sticky note and stuck it to the side of the shower so that I would see them as my mind started to thaw out and begin processing thoughts again. It is kind of like journaling right when you wake up from a dream because you know you won't remember much of it in a couple of hours.

I wanted those questions to be the first things I recognized as my focus started dialing back in, and, after a while, I started defining the gray area.

It happened much faster than I imagined it would too. It wasn't an overnight thing, but within a few weeks of doing this intentionally, I had enough definition in the gray to start making some remarkably impactful moves in my life.

The Primal Method was born, and it evolved very fast.

With that said, here is my six-layered strategy for optimal preparedness in the modern age. The gray area is defined. It's a sequential, practical, dynamic, building-block style system that you can apply to your life no matter where you live, what your age is, how much money you have, or where you get your training.

Are you ready?

CHAPTER 15

Layer 1 - Foundations

Where everyone should begin, but most people finish. This is backward, and it needs to be corrected if true preparedness is your goal.

It all starts by getting right spiritually. God & Jesus Christ are the substrate of substrates. The foundation of foundations. From God, all else is created. You will build a full life and still feel an emptiness in the end if you neglect this. It's a gray zone that needs definition. You can be perfect at everything I explain in this book, but if you skip this aspect, I believe that none of it will truly matter in the long run.

You may feel objective to this ideal, and that's okay. You have that freedom. If you think you need to forgo this step of the process, I understand.

All I am going to say on this aspect is that I have concluded that if you do everything else I tell you in this book, but omit this one single part, don't be surprised if you still have a lot of voids and gray areas in your life in the end. If you don't, great, but if you do, I suggest following the method in its entirety.

Faith plays a critical role in this game.

Having faith requires us to trust something we don't fully understand. We can calculate our moves as thoroughly as possible, but no matter what, there's always going to be some questions we won't be able to answer in this life.

It's no debate that these unanswerable questions create a big void in our lives, and we are programmed with a desire to understand it.

I don't believe it's possible, though, not in this life at least.

This endeavor to answer all of the questions creates a barrier between peace in our lives.

I think if we were given all the answers, it would honestly melt our brains. The only way I found to truthfully fill that void and find some peace was to place my faith in God. This doesn't mean to stop questioning things or seeking the answers, though. We couldn't stop no matter how bad we wanted to. There's always going to be an instinctual hunger for the answers. If we look at the history of the world, we know this to be true.

We can "fast" or abstain from questioning as many times as we want, but the hunger for answers will always win at the end of the day. This doesn't mean we can't be at peace along the way, though.

Faith in God won't take away the questions or give you all the answers, but true faith can and will bring you peace, and peace is paramount for productively overcoming these obstacles we're about to talk about.

Without peace, you will struggle much more than necessary. This much I will promise.

Suppose you struggle with doing this. I understand, we all do, and we always will. So this is why I'm going to tell you that I firmly believe you need to do this, and at the same time, I understand if you can't right now or think that you never could.

I will not condemn you to any fate.

I am only a human being.

I don't have those kinds of divine powers.

With all that said, to reach optimal preparedness, you need to be squared away. While I believe God is more than capable of clearing the fog for us, I also think he places certain things into our hands so that we may learn some valuable lessons about this life he has given us.

That's enough on this aspect, though. There is another book out there incomparably more profound than this one if you would like to understand more on this specific aspect of preparedness.

It's called the Holy Bible, and I encourage you to read it before committing to applying my additional methods to your life.

I hope you understand my view and reasoning for all of this. If you do, outstanding. If you don't and wish to, please feel free to reach out, and we can discuss it personally.

Moving on...

You see, much like a house, you can't expect to hold up to the test of time without having a strong foundation. This layer is primarily focused on developing a hardened mindset and strategy for life and a well-rounded understanding of it.

Your gear, survival skills, and weapons training mean very little if you come home to broken relationships, a career that doesn't support your dreams, or finances that don't allow you the freedom to live.

None of the "cool stuff" matters if you come home at the end of the day to a life you hate living.

In this layer, the objective is to square every bit of that away so you can begin to build a solid house of preparedness.

It's important to reverse engineer processes to understand better how things work, and that's precisely what I did to create the sequence of The Primal Method itself. I looked at it from the perspective of what's holding me back from accomplishing my objectives now. When we think about it practically, we can start to see the building block process reveal itself. You can do this to overcome virtually any problem in your life.

Now, I believe the foundation is the most critical aspect of all this. That's why it gets the most attention, the largest piece of the pie, if you will.

You will face many obstacles in life, but I have narrowed it down to eight core areas. If you can overcome these eight challenges, you will have a rock-solid foundation to build from. If these obstacles are present in your life, it creates an overwhelming amount of brain fog. So much fog that it will make the path ahead of you unnavigable.

This is where seeking mentors who have been there and done that becomes helpful. I followed their trail markers, and slowly, I was able to clear the fog in my life over many years.

Instead of leaving simple trail markers myself, I decided to dig deep into why the fog was there in the first place so that I could pave a clear path and eliminate it much faster for my kids and anyone else who chooses to adopt my methods. I want to shave down the learning curve and help people obtain freedom and happiness.

Many people have created tactics to overcome the obstacles we're about to dive into. My ways are not the only ways, and I will never claim them to be, but I know that they are incredibly efficient.

So, let's reverse engineer these obstacles you will face when trying to optimize your life and build this foundation. We will systematically clear this fog so you can see the trail and become ridiculously productive at climbing this mountain of life.

Be warned, though.

Overcoming these obstacles is going to take a massive amount of work.

Knowing the trail doesn't necessarily mean it makes it easier to hike it. It just means you know where you're headed. Take comfort in that fact, but get ready to grind harder than ever.

There's no cheat codes in this game, only instruction manuals. Some are better than others, and I strongly believe in the one I have created for you here. Sure, I'm a little biased, but I am also making this declaration on the back of a boatload of testimonials.

So, let's dive into the obstacles.

CHAPTER 16

Obstacle 1 - The Blueprint

Who you plan to become.

It probably doesn't come as a surprise when I say that most people don't have a tactical plan for their life. A vague one typically exists, but usually, it's only floating around in their mind. I lived this way for an extended portion of my life. At some point, you have to stop winging it if you want to make it to new levels in the game, though.

Please don't wait until rock bottom as I did. If you do, there's a 50/50 chance you might not get another chance. So, If you're winging life right now, I need you to flip that fucking switch immediately. Trust me when I say that it's vital to have a serious plan and work it to get results. Let this be your signal.

Please allow these words to resonate within your soul.

THAT MOMENT YOU'RE WAITING ON FOR IT TO FEEL PERFECT ISN'T COMING.

I will try my best, but nobody is coming to save you at the end of the day. Adopt this mindset right here and now. There may be people like me who help guide you throughout the journey, but in the end, it's just you. You're the only one that can do the work. You are the one who has to decide to move, and if you ever plan on being the lighthouse for anyone else in life, you must first get to shore yourself.

Planning is the first step because taking action without a clear objective doesn't make sense. You need to have a clearly identified target before you shoot. You need to know your heading before you set sail.

So, I reverse-engineered the problem and asked myself, *"What's holding me back from success right now?"*

It boiled down to the lack of a proper plan.

I also discovered this to be a consistent obstacle with all of my students over the years. The ones who were suffering the most didn't have plans at all. Even the ones who sometimes appeared to have their shit together didn't have a real plan more often than not.

Once I made this connection, I determined that the first step to an optimized lifestyle was to develop the blueprint—the outline for who you desire to become. It's a life plan that specifies your passions and purpose, code of conduct, visions, possessions, etc. It's your very identity—the life you wish to live, designed, and defined in detail. The first part of constructing any building is to create the blueprint. A blueprint for life is more of a description of what you want it to look like than it is a giant checklist of goals.

Keep that in mind when you start designing.

CHAPTER 17

Obstacle 2 - The War Plan

How you plan to get there.

This step is a little more difficult as the planning process for it can get very extensive. It all depends on how ambitious you are with the blueprint.

Once you have your blueprint, you can create the war plan. The blueprint is who you plan to be; the war plan is how you're going to become that person. I call it war planning because, let's face it, we live life on a battlefield. War planning is a unique process that I created. It's not as simple as making some lists and checking them twice. This isn't your Christmas list for Santa. This is the plan you will use to triumph over your enemies in life.

Remember, enemies are anyone or anything that stands between you and the fulfillment of your purpose.

I tried to use every version of a higher performance planning system out there. I used paper planners; I used digital apps, whiteboards, and virtually everything you can think of; nothing ever satisfied me. Much like I couldn't find a solution for the void, I couldn't find a proper solution for planning either, so I created one.

The problem I had with most planning tools is that they're too specific to the person who designed them. This means you might struggle to use it for your life. After all, It was designed for someone else's.

When I set out to create the solution, I kept this problem at the forefront of my mind. I wanted to create a well rounded, but most importantly, adaptable system that would work for virtually anyone's life, from average Joe to CEO. It started as a paper process, then evolved into a digital one, but I won't be diving into the details of how this war planning process works here.

However, if you would like to get started with the basics now, you can use the totally free, interactive paper war planners that I created. It will show you the process in its simplest form. Again, they're completely free, and I genuinely hope you use them. You can find the War Planners on our website, and I've dropped a handful of helpful links at the end of this book.

Once you master the basic version of the war planning process, you can become a student of our training course called Operation Optimize, where I teach the advanced digital version of the process and provide a template that will change your life.

You can certainly use other tools and processes and get results. I think you'll find it easier to get them with ours, though. At the end of the day, the most important thing is creating the plan in general.

The tool you use to produce it doesn't matter so much.

A blueprint is pointless without a war plan, and a war plan is meaningless without a blueprint. These two things go hand in hand.

Abraham Lincoln said, *"Give me six hours to chop down a tree, and I will spend the first four sharpening the axe."*

Your plan is the axe.

CHAPTER 18

Obstacle 3 - Taking Action

When you plan to execute.

Now that you have a blueprint and a war plan, the next thing you need to do is figure out when to execute. When reverse engineering, I discovered that the next thing that held me back from the massive success I wanted was proper *time management.*

It's been said that *"A goal without a plan is just a wish."* I also think a plan without a deadline *echos* that.

If it's not on your schedule, it doesn't genuinely exist, and it's probably never going to be accomplished. A great deal of people make plans but never actually schedule a time for executing them.

Time management is a vital skill set that I think everyone should spend more time practicing.

After you know who you want to be and how you're going to become that person, you need to learn how to control and manage your time appropriately. Changing into this new person and getting the results you want will require massive amounts of work. So, when do you plan for this work to get done?

You can accomplish this allocation of time with virtually any calendaring tool, but like most things, I have a preferred tool and unique strategies. You can learn more about them and all of these obstacles in layer one, for that matter, inside our tribe, and Operation Optimize specifically.

You can find what works for you or follow in my footsteps. Again, what matters most is that you have these plans in place. You can overcome every one of these obstacles for free if you want to. However, we provide the tools that can help you do it more efficiently, which will give you back more of your precious time.

CHAPTER 19

Obstacle 4 - Energy

Combating the inevitable exhaustion from taking massive action.

At this point in building your foundation, you have determined who you want to be, how you will become that person, and when you will execute. The next thing that's going to stand in your way is your energy. After you execute for a while, you will get tired. You must try to source your energy from natural, beneficial methods.

Pounding coffee and energy drinks is not healthy or sustainable, and it's not an optimal way to live. If you do it long enough, you will crash and burn, and it will negate all of the hard work you put in on obstacles 1-3.

How did you feel when you woke up this morning?

Think about it.

Did you feel happy and full of energy? Did you feel excited and ready to tackle the day, or did you feel tired and stressed out?

Did you have anxiety about all the stuff you have to do today? Did you want to burrow back into the covers and sleep all day?

The tone you set in the morning has considerable influence over the rest of your day. How you go to sleep also plays a significant factor in how you wake too. The main problem is that most people wake up in reaction mode. When the alarm goes off in the morning, they're already hitting the snooze button, starting the day in a reactive state.

After they oversleep and rush to get ready for the day, they feel unmotivated, unproductive, and stressed out, surrounded by everything they have to get done.

They have to have a coffee for a boost of energy because they're still tired even though they got in their eight hours of sleep. Then they consume an unhealthy breakfast because they're in a rush, and they rinse and repeat this same process day in and day out.

We can't always control what happens in life, but we can control how we react to it. You need to wake up each day in a proactive state versus a reactive state. This comes down to the first decision you make when you wake up. You can choose something intentionally that will give you a boost, or you can reactively select something that will drain you. This choice is up to you.

You have control over this.

Let me ask you, what if there was a way you could consciously kick off your day in a proactive state? What if you could start waking up each day with passion, energy, and a fire inside your soul?

What if you woke up excited, happy, and took the time to prime yourself for optimal performance each day? How different would your day look? How different would your life be? Well, you can accomplish this with discipline and the right daily energy rituals. This means having a strategic set of empowering habits that you can do throughout the day to set yourself up for success. It won't remove all the bad days entirely, obviously, but it will help you have more good ones consistently.

You see, after years and years of following top entrepreneurs, athletes, and high performers, one thing I've found common amongst most of them is that they have powerful morning rituals. I like to call them daily energy rituals because while they're most potent in the morning, you can do them throughout the day when you start feeling off your game. I've been doing energy rituals for years now, and I can see dramatic differences in my productivity if I don't do them.

I've used these energy rituals to help create the life I want.

They help me make more money, help me with my health and fitness, and even help me cultivate better relationships. Not only that, but they've also helped me build businesses, enrich my mindset, and much more. Most importantly, they keep me in a near-constant flow state where I'm the most productive I can be, and being in this flow state is a key to optimal performance.

Powerful daily rituals can change your life **dramatically**.

My question to you now is, what does your current routine look like?

Proactive or reactive, we perform rituals every day, and these rituals have a major influence on our future actions. If we wake up doing our natural reactive routines, we condition ourselves to be late, stressed, tired, depressed, and ultimately stuck. However, we can design the rituals we are performing, and if we wake up proactive, we can manifest what we desire most in life.

If you've made it this far, you have a new ideal lifestyle by your design and a complete system for managing all of your goals, projects, time, and tasks. I've explained how to become productive; now, it's time to stay in that productive state.

Pick your energy rituals wisely and put time on your calendar to practice them throughout the day. Things like chanting affirmations, looking at vision boards, breathwork, reviewing your war plans, or knocking out a quick set of pushups are great things.

David Goggins might say to reach into the *"cookie jar"* or stare into the *"accountability mirror."* These are great tactics too.

There are tons of powerful rituals you can use. Even something as simple as smiling can dramatically change your mood. Don't believe me? Pause for a moment and force a smile for me.

It sounds silly, I know, but trust me.

You might not feel it at first, but things start to feel better if you do it long enough. It attracts good vibes, and this will give you some clean energy to move forward. I like to start my day with a smile. It's the easiest proactive thing I can do to have a positive impact on my morning.

Most people roll over, moan and groan, check emails, or scroll their social media news feeds. It doesn't take long doing this before you get slapped in the face with attacks from haters or become depressed from all the evil going on around the world.

This is a **dangerous** ritual to have. It sucks your energy away.

You've got to get your mind right, especially first thing in the morning, if you'd like to have a productive and happy day. So, be intentional and live proactively, not reactively. Next time you feel sluggish, perform a clean energy ritual. Don't chug a coffee or Redbull. I'm not saying you should never do these things. You can use them in certain situations. Just be sure that these situations actually demand them and that you have exhausted your natural energy hacks first.

CHAPTER 20

Obstacle 5 - Self Sabotage

How to silence the most prominent critic you will ever have,
yourself.

This one defeats a lot of people. Once you know who you want to be, how you're going to get there, when you're going to execute, and how to keep your energy strong and clean, the next thing that will prevent your success is your self-doubt. Honestly, this is probably the one I struggled with the most. Before I got optimized, I used to believe in others' opinions to the point that it defined who I was.

I was a picture painted by all the teachers, friends, family members, and haters that told me I was destined for failure growing up.

I heard that shit so much that I had started to believe it. I didn't want to, but at the time, I didn't know how to become more than that.

Who we surround ourselves with and what we allow into our ears and eyes has a significant impact on who we are. Once I learned this, I started to clean up my circle and sphere of influence consciously.

Cleaning up your environment isn't the only way to overcome self-doubt, though. There are some very tactical ways to defeat it.

I teach them to our students in Operation Optimize, but I'll extend this critical lesson to you. You see, when it comes to achievement, two things continuously battle in our brains.

DOUBT AND ACTION

Doubt, if you let it consume you, will get you nowhere. On the other hand, action will take you as far, wide, and high as you can imagine.

Doubt and action cannot co-exist in the same space. That's why it's a constant war in our minds. We obviously don't want doubt to win, so how can we consistently defeat it?

I'm going to let you in on a little secret...

Your doubts are afraid of your actions.

It's a fantastic feeling when you can operate without an abundance of doubt. The more action you take, the further self-doubt runs. When you occupy your entire mind with massive effort, doubt can't exist. So, the key to defeating doubt is to take action. If you're sitting around, if you're idle, if you're enjoying an unearned nap, that's when doubt walks back in the frame.

If you have time to doubt, you have time to take action. Doubting yourself is easy and easy leads to ordinary. Taking action is hard but leads to extraordinary. If the majority of your life consists of massive action and you stay very disciplined with it, doubt will get tired of having nowhere to hang and stop trying to come over so often.

So yes, you can take breaks. Just make sure you've earned them. If you don't earn it, doubt's going to come knocking.

The main thing I fear in life is not relentlessly pursuing to be the greatest I can be to contribute to this world in the most significant way I can.

We all have these two sides...

One tells us to be average because it's secure and balanced. The other tells us to be great because it's free and full of life. I live in fear of that average part of me. He's always there and is always telling me how much easier it would be just to quit, and he never leaves.

He conveniently fails to remind me of the pain I'd eventually come to feel from his ordinary vision. That's what I'm always reminded of by the part of me that craves greatness, the pain. I don't want to live my life in pain, and I would venture to say that you don't either.

Settling and letting your average self take control results in security. It wraps you up in chains and puts you in prison.

Building an empire might bring you to the brink of death, but you will forever be free if you manage to build it.

What side of you will you let prevail?

Ordinary you, or extraordinary you?

That's why I created my alter ego, *"Primal."* He's the me I wish to become. I do my best to summon him every day because he's obsessed with massive action and destroys self-doubt with ease.

I like to think that Primal is God's unique way of communicating with me since I was too stubborn to listen to him any other way growing up. He knew I only trusted myself, so he had me create a version of myself that I would listen to.

There are more tactics for preventing this self-sabotage, but this concept of action versus doubt will completely change the game for you. You don't have to create an alter ego. This is just the strategy I use, and it helps me a lot.

Taking massive action is all you need to focus on if you want to eliminate your doubts. If you feel any doubt, that's the indicator you need to pay attention to. When you feel the doubt, commence the actions as soon as possible, no matter how big or little they may seem.

Remember, sometimes, that action is as simple as a smile.

CHAPTER 21

Obstacle 6 - Health 101

Being healthy is a critical aspect of the foundation. You need to understand the basics of health to free yourself of illness and mitigate injury.

The next thing that will take you out of the fight is your physical fitness. You don't need to be a freak athlete when it comes to the foundation, though. You need to simply understand the fundamentals of what health is and how to achieve it.

Health is defined as *"the state of being free from illness or injury."*

Those are the two things that will prevent you from success next because, at this point, you know who you want to be, how you're going to get there, when you're going to execute, and how to keep your energy strong and clean for the journey. At this level of optimizing your life, it means understanding health well enough to stay free from illness or injury.

Neglect this area for long, and you can bank on sickness or broken bones to put your ass on the bench with a quickness.

Once more, the objective during this stage isn't to build the body of a gladiator. It's to be healthy, and it doesn't take an extreme understanding to accomplish this. Get healthy because if you don't, you probably won't fulfill the plans you're going to work so hard to create.

Also, bear in mind, sometimes you won't feel the effects of bad decisions for years. Not eating right or working out will take a severe toll on you, and you won't even realize it till you get put in the hospital.

Don't wait for the scare. A healthy body is essential for a strong preparedness foundation.

It would help if you also considered learning basic first aid skills at this level. The ability to provide at least basic first aid to yourself and others in the absence of a medical pro is invaluable. It's also another highly neglected aspect of preparedness.

If everyone else dropped the ball or weren't there when you needed them, you at least need to be able to mend basic wounds on your own.

This doesn't mean you need to become a doctor; it just means you need to learn the fundamentals.

Situational awareness is also something critical to develop and practice during layer one. Situational awareness alone can prevent many headaches and potentially unhealthy events. Be sure to check out some of the related training guides on these topics on our website as it goes much deeper than "keeping your head on a swivel."

CHAPTER 22

Obstacle 7 - Relationships

Many have said, "your network is your net worth." The next thing that will hold you back is the company you keep.

Digging deeper into what held me back, I found that my relationships played a huge factor. Not just between my family and me, but also with my friends, fans, tribe members, or clients. Relationships are interesting because not only do they have an ability to hold you back, they can also provide ample opportunities to propel you forward.

You don't know what you don't know, but someone you know might know someone who does, and that person might be the key to a new door in your life. You never honestly know. Networking is such a powerful thing.

Think about it.

If you had never opened this book, you might not have developed this relationship with me now. That would be unfortunate because you would have never learned this incredible method for total life preparedness.

I'm so glad you did, though, truly.

It adds some serious fuel to my fire and makes me excited for what you'll do next.

The right relationships nurtured correctly can add a great deal of joy to your life. However, the wrong relationships can drag you down, and sometimes it doesn't matter how you nurture them. My best advice for developing positive relationships is through adding value to people, being transparent, and becoming the lighthouse that guides people home.

Attraction is a powerful tool.

Be attractive.

We are products of our environment. Like I said before, who and what we surround ourselves with has a massive influence on the way we live, and in turn, the results we get.

Optimal living at this point will require you to develop positive relationships and cut off ones that are harmful to you. This means you might need to have some difficult and possibly painful conversations with people who are very close to you, but you must do it.

Please know that I and everyone in the tribe will be here to help you navigate this sketchy terrain.

CHAPTER 23

Obstacle 8 - Finances

If you have above-average ambitions, they will be fueled by the business you build, or they won't be realized at all. At this point, you've created your personal brand. It's time to convert it into a business.

At this level of the game, we have reached what I consider to be the icing on the foundational cake. Depending on your ambition level, the next obstacle that will hold you back is a financial one.

When you reach this point in your optimization journey, you have accomplished quite a few things. So far, we have designed the blueprint, devised the war plan, and determined when we will execute it.

Beyond that, we have also learned to keep our energy levels high to stay productive, crush self-doubt, get healthy, and improve our relationships.

When you arrive here, the only thing preventing you from success by most people's definition will be your career. How you make your money. You need to make sure it supports your blueprint. Standard jobs and careers will only yield a standard lifestyle, and I think you're here because you want more than that. If not, and you're truly at peace with average, I'm okay with that, but I hope you're here for more.

If a typical 9-5 will sustain your visions, then that's completely okay. If it won't, that's where you will need to invest in the idea of creating your own business. You could even take advantage of our business opportunities through our Vanguard program to make this happen. Still, either way, you need something that can create additional income to support this ultimate lifestyle you designed. If you don't, this is the last major thing that can hold you back from success.

These are the eight obstacles of growth that I discovered through my journey of optimizing my life and helping our students get optimized. It's also important to understand that life optimization and improvement to your foundation is a never-ending process.

I'm continually sharpening these tools and finding new ways to optimize the way I live and so should you.

These obstacles are not the only obstacles you may face, just the major ones. Thankfully, now you have some actionable advice and insight on overcoming them when they arise.

Please do not neglect your foundation, my friend.

It's the most critical layer of this entire process.

CHAPTER 24

Layer 2 - Fitness

Transitioning the body from average to savage.

Moving forward in The Primal Method, the next logical and practical step is to advance your health & fitness. Now, I mentioned these things in layer one, but that was for the basics. In layer two, it's about becoming strong and even more capable.

Strength is such a critical part of life, and there's much to be said about the benefits of intentionally putting yourself through uncomfortable physical challenges. Not only will you grow stronger physically, but you will also enhance your mind and ability to think and perform more proficiently. Think of this layer as a performance enhancing supplement to layer one.

None of the gun fighting, shelter building, and fire-making skills will make a big difference if you can't run a mile without feeling like you're going to die.

In this layer, you should work on your nutrition and workout routines to develop a savage body because a savage body will enhance the mind's performance.

This is the next logical step after pouring your foundation in layer one. It's time to build the frame for your house of preparedness.

Sometimes the best thing you can do to overcome a rut in life is to get out of your head and get into your body. These two systems work hand in hand, and we have to keep them running smoothly if we want great results in the long run.

Physical fitness is also the gateway to building your mental discipline. In the military, this was at the core of everything. Even things we typically brush off, such as making our beds. Failure to do this and your leadership is going to smoke you out physically.

This physical punishment enforces the importance of being mentally disciplined down to the fundamental things in life. The things we feel aren't super important are what actually make all the difference at scale. These seemingly minor things are the initial rocks we throw in the water.

These rocks create a ripple effect, and how big the rocks are, is what will determine if the ripples turn into waves or dissipate into nothing.

Want to make bigger waves? Become disciplined with the "small" things and execute them consistently.

Want to get more disciplined? Seek out physical challenges. Stop trying to think more discipline into your life. Discipline comes from strong faith and a self-created fear of physical discomfort.

Discomfort forces us to move, remember?

CHAPTER 25

Layer 3 - Unarmed Combatives

Becoming the weapon.

Your mind and body have been hardened to withstand the test of time, and your life is squared away. The next logical step in your preparedness is to become a weapon to defend yourself and those around you. Before learning how to use weapons, though, you must learn how to become a weapon.

Again, The Primal Method is about preparing for the highest priority threats first. Home invasions, active shooters, rape attacks, human traffickers, or hostile environments following natural disasters.

These are the things that we must be ready for today.

Unless you live deep in the uncharted wilderness, these evils are genuine and increasing day by day. This is why, for the majority of the world, hand to hand combative skills would prove more useful in the modern age than primitive shelter building skills.

While they are both critical, one is statistically more likely to be needed today for most of us.

So, before we learn to fight with guns and knives, we learn to fight with our bodies. If you can shoot a gun but can't throw hands, there's something a little backward with how you're preparing yourself.

Learning martial arts is a very beneficial thing, and it goes well beyond the skills you learn. Martial arts has an impressive way of humbling you. The more you learn, the more you spar, the more you roll, the more wise and peaceful you become. It, too, builds discipline because it is an extension of your fitness. It also intensifies self-awareness. It's a very physically demanding task that stems from a great understanding of fundamental principles.

One of my favorite quotes from a man who had arguably the most well-rounded understanding of unarmed combatives a person could have is…

"I fear not the man who has practiced 10,000 kicks once, but I fear the man who has practiced one kick 10,000 times." - Bruce Lee

The greatest fighters in the world have outstanding mental discipline levels and consistently focus on their fundamentals over flash.

Another significant aspect of training martial arts is the relationships you build. Nothing bonds people better than combat. There's just something unique about it. My best friends are the people I have suffered through intense physical challenges and trained combatives with, and when it comes to preparedness, these skill sets will help you mitigate a plethora of potential threats.

CHAPTER 26

Layer 4 - Armed Combatives

Pick up a force multiplier, and put a swift end to the threat.

Now that you have become a weapon from layer three, you can enhance your ability to fight with force-multiplying tools such as guns, blades, sticks, spears, bows, etc.

Pretty much anything.

The real world has no rules, and your enemies will use whatever they can to harm you.

There's no such thing as a fair fight in the real world, so you need to learn how to maintain the advantage to ensure your survival.

Many people own weapons but rarely invest in training to learn how to use them properly. Don't be most people.

Learn how to be effective with your tools, and take good care of them; that way, they'll take good care of you if they're ever called to action.

Everyone's area has different laws and regulations surrounding the use of these kinds of tools. Please follow them, and work within your scope of legal abilities. If you are restricted from certain things, you should still invest in learning what you can about how to use them or acquire them in the event of any kind of WROL (Without Rule Of Law) situation.

Another mindset I believe in firmly is that if you want to carry the tools to take a life, please also have the tools and knowledge you may need to save them. You never know. You might need to use them to save yours in the unpreferred event that you or someone you love becomes the victim.

CHAPTER 27

Layer 5 - Prepping

Specifically, the accumulation of supplies and resources and the knowledge and skills for creating and sustaining them.

Now that the mind and body are savage, and you know how to defend yourself, your family, and those around you from the higher priority threats, it's time to prepare for tough times.

This layer is all about building up your defenses and self-sustainment supplies and resources.

From the storage of gear, medical supplies, food, and water, to the setup of alternative energy systems, prepping is about never being in the position to need and not have.

In this stage, you need to learn as much as you can about your gear, cybersecurity, home defense, communications, homesteading, blacksmithing, woodworking, etc. Learn how to create it yourself should you not be able to acquire it through normal channels. You need to become the epitome of the word *"resourceful."*

Need a knife but can't afford one or find one?

Learn how to make one.

Need food but can't afford much?

Learn how to grow it.

Need a backpack or blanket?

Learn how to sew.

You get my point.

Trade skills like these are advantageous, no matter what era we are living in. If everything collapses around you, they become invaluable.

If we can build a castle, supply it, and defend it well, chances are we should be able to weather any severe siege that comes our way.

Bugging out is always a last resort option.

The last thing you want to do is leave behind this arsenal that you have spent years of your life and thousands of dollars building.

Along with this building of your castle and defenses, you should also develop your network of allies. Your network is a valuable resource, as well. It can help you fill the gaps in your defensive perimeter while you're building things up.

Do not approach this as a lone wolf.

CHAPTER 28

Layer 6 - Operational Skills

Mission-oriented skill sets and tactics that enhance your survivability in dangerous, hostile, or primitive environments, whether it's the urban city or the wild wilderness.

When it comes to this word "*survival,*" most people picture a man running in the jungle, building friction fires, shelters, and eating raw fish with his bare hands. While this is cool, it's not the reality in the modern world.

There are very few societies still living this primitive way, and some even do so by choice. However, these skills are still very vital for your preparedness.

The problem is that this is where most people begin. They grab a bug out bag and start learning how to make fires and build shelters while they neglect their foundations or fitness.

They are preparing for lower priority threats, and that's the very reason why I created The Primal Method.

I wanted to give people a logical system to follow.

Now that you have the skills to defend, a hardened mind and body, and the preps to keep you going, the objective is serious operational skill-building: bushcraft, Tradecraft, Fieldcraft, and Advanced First Aid.

Now, most people with any mind for preparedness are familiar with the term "*bushcraft*," but not so many know about tradecraft and fieldcraft. At a glance, one might assume they all mean the same general thing, but there are some distinct differences.

With **bushcraft**, the meaning is simply the art of living in the bush—wilderness/primitive skill sets. You know, friction fires, shelters, trapping, hunting, tracking, etc.

Tradecraft is the cool guy stuff we see in movies like Jason Bourne or James Bond.

The art of espionage (spying). Learning how to disappear and hide in plain sight. Another word or phrase you might hear relating to this craft is *"Gray Man."*

Fieldcraft pertains mostly to the art of stealth operation and the various methods to do so regardless of the weather, terrain, or time of day/night.

Fieldcraft skill sets include water and land navigation, camouflage, understanding cover versus concealment, efficient observation, countersurveillance, survival, escape, and evasion tactics.

Skills that you typically don't learn about outside of the military.

All of these crafts can be extremely fun to build and learn. I can understand the draw to them. However, the average civilian is typically never in the kind of environment that would be practical for these particular skill sets. Of them all, bushcraft is probably the most likely to be needed for most people.

As you already know, though, there are greater threats for most of us than getting lost in the woods with minimal or no gear. Which leads me to the meaning of *"Operational."*

Operational, in this context, means **mission-oriented**. It means having a planned mission versus an unplanned emergency response to a situation.

With layers 3-4, we speak about armed and unarmed combatives. Two skill sets that could very well be considered operational too, but unless it's your actual job, they are looked at through the lens of self-defense.

Such as an active shooter popping off in the food court while you're eating with your family, a home invader breaking in while you're asleep one night, or the aggressive asshole at the bar.

These are *self-defense* scenarios unless you're a first responder.

Now, If you're a military asset with a mission to eliminate a specific target, or a paramedic assigned the task to save someone that got shot during an armed robbery, that's different. These would be what I consider *"Operational"* scenarios. The job demanded it and gave you a specific mission to execute.

Now, why is all this operational/mission talk relevant?

It's relevant because all of these particular skill sets mitigate the average individual's lowest priority threats. Most people are just rarely ever going to be in a situation that demands these skills for survival.

This doesn't mean they're not necessary, though. You should absolutely train these skill sets. You just need to ensure that you're not training them at the expense of other, more critical, skills that mitigate higher priority threats.

Especially if you are weak in those sectors.

Train where you are weakest concerning your highest priority threat.

Depending on your job, your health, geography, etc. You might be at abnormal risk levels for specific lower priority threats, according to the data. You might be an exception. It's vital to figure this out first before you start applying this method to your life.

Again, *train where you are weakest concerning your highest priority threat*.

I designed The Primal Method based on death statistics. So, if you're not at abnormal risk for something, you can follow the method as it's structured, and it will help you get prepared for the highest priority threats first.

So, besides the few people whose job or environment demands high proficiency in these types of skill sets to survive, layer 6 comes last because, for most people, it's unlikely to be in a situation that requires these skills for survival in the modern age.

PRIMAL'S WAR JOURNAL

DATE: OCT. 16TH 2017
SUBJECT: BACK TO THE BASICS

The infamous "rut." We search high and low for a sweet scientific solution, a secret strategy perhaps... Something we possibly overlooked throughout the journey that could pull us back into that uber-productive flow state that we were accustomed to.

Thing is... what we were doing didn't just magically stop working to bring about this rut. The reality is that we stopped doing the work. The plan was working, and the results were flowing. The best way to get back to that is to get back to the basics.

The little monotonous tasks. The small, but massively essential details that we struggle to maintain consistency in. The plan never stopped working, we just stopped working the plan, and now, we must get back to the basics and stop looking for the magic fix. It doesn't exist, and the sooner you accept that the faster the rut will end, and you can begin to move the needle again.

SECTION VII: A SHIFT IN PERSPECTIVE

CHAPTER 29

The Strategy

You now know the layers and why they exist. Let's step back and take a look at the big picture to understand The Primal Method preparedness machine at scale.

For most, It's only going to be after you have *"bugged out"* and left your resources that you genuinely need layer six skills to survive. Chances of this happening are slim for the majority. It's still a variable we prepare for; it's just not as pressing as the other things we've discussed.

This is why prepping comes before survival, why armed combatives come before prepping, why unarmed combatives come before armed combatives, why fitness comes before unarmed combatives, and why the foundation comes before everything.

We must face the force with a strong posture.

You see, It's easy to get pushed down when you're standing normal and upright. It's not so easy if you stagger your legs, bend the knees, and lean into the force. Life and mother nature are the purest forms of formidable forces to exist.

Preparedness is the ability to face these forces with the right posture.

Don't want to get knocked down? Build your house on top of a solid foundation, and posture yourself correctly for the modern world's threats.

My mission is to help you do precisely that with a guided, practical purpose.

The solutions that existed before this didn't make as much sense to me. They didn't fill the voids, define the gray zones, or bridge the gaps.

Reverse engineering is a great way to find solutions to problems, and preparing backward was a problem I discovered, so I wanted to create a solution. Not just for my preparedness journey, but everyone else's too. Preparedness isn't something we're taught in school. I want this book to serve that purpose and be the awakening of a new aged way of living a prepared life.

However, just because I have created this systematic approach to preparedness doesn't mean the puzzle is finished. You still need to make sure you are always conducting threat assessments.

Threats change, and therefore your training and the layer you are focusing on should adapt to what threatens your survival most. Once you prepare for those threats and mitigate them to the best of your abilities, you conduct another threat assessment and continue training and building your layers accordingly.

You need to be dynamic.

Remember, most of these skills are perishable. Neglect any layer for too long, and your percentage of effectiveness will decline, opening you up to those threats again.

Try to stay active and keep the tanks as full as you can.

Think of each layer like independent gas tanks that collectively power one giant preparedness machine. Each gas tank powers one of these six layers of defense. If you let the gas tank go empty, there goes your defensive perimeter against those types of threats.

It doesn't matter where you source your knowledge or training from either. You can still apply this approach. It would be wise if you tried to get the best knowledge and training you can, though. It will make a significant difference in how effective you are and how well the Primal Method works for you.

If you have a solid foundation and are not at risk for disease or suicide (layer one), you need to work on your strength and agility (layer two).

Being physically fit trickles into your ability to do everything else. Like I mentioned earlier, fitness is like the framework for your house.

Once you're all framed up, it's time to install the plumbing and electric, or in other words, Armed and Unarmed Combatives (layers 3-4).

Once you're capable of protecting and defending, you need to add your roof and drywall, or preps (layer five).

Accumulate the resources and supplies you need to sustain you long term. From there, you build up your Operational Skills (Layer six).

PRIMAL'S WAR JOURNAL

DATE: DEC. 16TH 2018
SUBJECT: TRUTH HURTS BEFORE IT HELPS

Not always, but quite often, you'll notice people get incredibly defensive if you tell them a truth they don't want to hear.

If you're the wrong one, they will prove it. If not, they will typically get defensive and illogically justify the thing you called them out on. Sometimes even to the point of just flat out ignoring you. They will act like you're too stupid to understand and that you just don't get it.

Don't let this get under your skin. You know you're right because they have yet to present logical evidence that proves otherwise.

The truth will set you free, but not before it pisses you off or hurts your feelings. Remember this next time you default to defense when someone calls you out on something too. Defense mechanisms are natural reactions to attack. Be self-aware enough to evaluate yourself once the dust settles to see if you were wrong.

CHAPTER 30

The Next Step

Turning your gas into jet fuel.

My hope, at this point, is that there's a new spark of energy in your mind to take action, a new vision for life, as well as the understanding that preparedness is so much more than what most people initially perceive. If you want to be prepared, there's a much bigger picture to look at, and now, you have a strategy that makes sense. A method that should have been taught to us as kids but wasn't.

If you paid attention, you should know that knowledge doesn't mean skill. Your discovery of The Primal Method will not make you more prepared just by reading it. It will only be beneficial for you if you apply it and take massive action.

The next step is to conduct your threat assessment and start sourcing knowledge for each layer, focusing on where you are most vulnerable. Once you shore that up, proceed to follow the layered sequence as it's laid out for you. As you gain knowledge, hit the field and train it to translate it into the skills you need to mitigate the threats you face.

WHERE DO WE GO FROM HERE?

This is the point of the story where I need to make you an offer—an opportunity to turn your gas into jet fuel. I told you I was a solutions-oriented guy, right? I also told you in the beginning that we would see how serious you are about your preparedness at the end.

Not only did I create this method, but I also made The Warrior Tribe to back it. It's a community of prepared minds, and the Primal Method is at the core of it. You already learned the challenges and some of our solutions for them earlier in the book, but there's so much more to learn and experience.

This book is but the *gateway of so much more.*

I have one final question to leave you with, my friend, and that is...

WILL YOU JOIN US?

Now, before you decide, please know that joining the tribe is a serious commitment. If you join us, please know that we will challenge you in ways you've never been challenged before. We plan to actually help you get positive results in life and preparedness, not just talk about it and hype you up.

THIS IS AS REAL AS IT GETS.

Trust me when I say that if your tribe isn't challenging you properly, it will never change you for the better. *Ours will do both*, and it does it exceptionally well.

Our Warrior Tribe and training programs, built on top of The Primal Method, is the perfect amalgamation for optimal preparedness for the modern age.

There are so many more amazing benefits and solutions that we have created that I didn't even explain to you in this book. The most important thing that I wanted to accomplish with this book is educating you on this unique preparedness method.

Remember, while it's still important, at the end of the day, it doesn't matter where you source your training from to apply The Primal Method to your life. Joining our Warrior Tribe will, however, dramatically enhance every aspect of everything you have learned here.

It will give you a ***strategic advantage***.

It's essential to be quick to *take advantage of an advantage*—especially one of this magnitude. So, if you would like to join and learn more, I would love to bring you on board, and I'm very much looking forward to helping you grow.

Please see the last few pages in the book for more information on how to get involved.

PRIMAL'S WAR JOURNAL

DATE: APR. 19TH 2012
SUBJECT: DEFEATED LANGUAGE

You cannot speak words that insinuate doubt or destruction. Words like "hopefully," or phrases like "If this happens," work against you to attract the very things you wish to avoid most.

They inspire doubt and attract adverse outcomes. This shifts your focus from action and confidence to self-doubt and stagnation.

Don't conduct your day using defeated language; otherwise, the next day, you'll be defeated for real.

Command growth in your life, start by changing your language and thought patterns to reflect nothing but good. Think it, say it, do it, obtain it.

Some words might not seem harmful on the surface, and that's why we must look for depth in all things. You need to find the substance—the true meaning.

CHAPTER 31

Gratitude & Goodbye For Now

Words can't express it, but I will do my best to try.

The mission I am on is unique, formidable, and much more significant than myself. I have not created these amazing things on my own, and I know I never could. So, for anyone to support the work we are doing by becoming a member, buying a book, training course, or sharing our content, *It truly means a lot.*

There aren't words that could describe the deep levels of gratitude that I feel if you have read this far, and I hope that this information hits you as profoundly as it did me when I had the epiphany that created it.

I also want to let you know that I am always available for anyone interested in learning more about anything in this book. If you have questions or need help with anything, please do not hesitate to ask. Unlike most people, when they say that, I genuinely mean it.

So, at this point, I guess it's time to say farewell. . .

I want to wish you great success throughout your life and journey to preparedness.

I hope this book will aid you in your endeavors.

Now get up, and go wage war, my friend.

I'll see you on the trail.

Bellum Gerere
   - *Ian "Primal" Talbert*

PRIMAL'S WAR JOURNAL

DATE: JAN. 1ST 2020
SUBJECT: EXECUTION

Society is moving so fast. Execution is more important now than it's ever been. If you think you have time to wait, you're wrong. There are probably hundreds of other people actively working on that thing you keep wishing you could build.

You don't have time to sit on the plan and wait for the perfect day.

It's not coming.

What will come is a day when your competition emerges, delivers, and kills your dreams.

Parallel thinking is real. If you think you're the only person with an idea... just sit around and think on it for a couple years and see if someone else doesn't come along and steal it from you.

Get to work.

And get to work yesterday.

EXTRA RESOURCES

Here is a list of our valuable resources that you can take

advantage of next.

JOIN THE WARRIOR TRIBE

WWW.MASKTACTICAL.COM/TRIBE

FREE WAR PLANNERS

WWW.MASKTACTICAL.COM/WAR-PLAN

OUR OFFICIAL TRAINING PROGRAMS

WWW.MASKTACTICAL.COM/TRAINING

THE INTELSECTOR (FREE BLOG CONTENT)

WWW.MASKTACTICAL.COM/INTEL-SECTOR

OUR YOUTUBE (FREE VIDEO CONTENT)

WWW.YOUTUBE.COM/MASKTACTICAL

LEARN MORE ABOUT US & OUR MISSION

WWW.MASKTACTICAL.COM

Additionally, If you would like to learn more about Ian or get in touch with him about collaborations, interviews, podcasts, consulting, speaking engagements, or anything else, please feel free to contact him directly through his personal website link below.

WWW.PRIMALOPTICS.COM

Made in the USA
Monee, IL
11 January 2021